THE BOOK OF
THE HOLY GRAAL

THE BOOK OF THE HOLY GRAAL *By* ARTHUR EDWARD WAITE

STONE GUILD PUBLISHING
PLANO, TEXAS
HTTP://WWW.STONEGUILDPUBLISHING.COM/

2009

Originally Published By:
J. M. WATKINS
1921

This Edition Copyright © 2008
Stone Guild Publishing, Inc.
Plano, Texas
http://www.stoneguildpublishing.com/

First Paperback Edition 2009

ISBN-13 978-1-60532-057-1
ISBN-10 1-60532-057-9

10 9 8 7 6 5 4 3 2

Contents

		PAGE
I	The Quest of a Perfect Sleep	7
II	Dream-Nomads	15
III	A Daughter of Life	21
IV	A Way in the Waking World	31
V	A Tale of Eternal Death	39
VI	The House of Many Mansions	47
VII	A Dream in the Quest of God	59
VIII	A Garden of Life	67
IX	The Master Comes	75
X	The Way of the Waterside	85
XI	Food of Heaven	93
XII	A Man and Maid	107
XIII	Of Spiritual Marriage	121
XIV	Priest and Priestess	135
XV	A Golden Veil of Doctrine	145
XVI	Christ Mystical	159
XVII	Within the Veil	165
XVIII	Valete	175

I

The Quest of a Perfect Sleep

SEEKERS of very life, who urge the quest,
    God save and keep you through the waking
        ways:
Hear ye the quest in dream. The soul is call'd
In every path and can advance in each.
God compasses His ends in ways of sleep,
As on death's road, and while from day to day
Light into dark dissolves, while night in turn
Dies and is glorified in golden dawn,
With no line drawn between, no mood of haste
Or violence: so softly, unawares—
After the wont of blessings—the sleep-state
And waking fuse together and transform.
Each unto each has ministry: the soul
Is led through both, and those who keep the quest—
Set round in all the spaces of the heart

With fires of eager longing—may in sleep
Press on to reach the vision and attain
The Sacred Goal.... Can dreams begun therein
Their true translation find in waking terms?
Where else but in high dream does quest begin—
Asleep and waking? Or when pass therefrom
But in the quickening and the eyes' keen light
Of compass'd end?
                     I look, my God, for Thee
On both sides of the world of life, and Thou
Hast peopled both with auspices, hast flung
Paths open. I have found Thy sacraments—
A daily nourishment—in each. Reverse
All normal orders, Thou forestalling Will:
One quest is ours; the ardent heart is one.
What care or choice is mine when all is Thou?
Nay, unto man I testify and Thee
That any phantom change which man calls death
Shall not one moment's space bewray the feet
Which hasten towards Thee. I have known one need
Since first we came together—Thou and I—
With that concurrent flash of certitude
That each was meant for each. The want is Thou.
Need me still, Master, on Thy part as God!
And slumber, waking life, concordant death,
Divided veils—showing another sun
Upon the soul—another mode of search,

THE QUEST OF A PERFECT SLEEP

Of questioning the darkness and the light
Until they give Thee up—not these, nor aught
Shall still or satisfy, or turn aside:
I challenge all in Thee, for Thee—the All.

Hear then the Quest in dream, and mark it well:
Sleep has its sacraments, and God pours through.
BEATA MEA through the world of dream
Went up and down in wistful ways of sleep,
And bore the great Pyx or Ciborium,
With meek hands lifted as in sacrifice,
Head as in worship bent. A crowd at times
She fed, with blessed fingers lifting up
Host after Host, pure lips from time to time
Blessing as well. Now some received, their hearts—
Like knees—inclined; some also bless'd; and some
Pray'd, in the presence of a mystery.
Some stood with heads erect, aspiring eyes,
Uplifted hands, as into rapture drawn,
Nor knew they well the giver or the gift,
By contemplation hush'd. But other some,
Heart-thankless, wrought with hunger, took and cursed.
Some cried, upbraiding; a few turn'd and rent
Their garments, passing into paths aside.
But whether dole or joy, the end was one:
From rapture, recollection or disdain

They rose, each man and woman going forth
Soul starved—O sorrowful, ungracious task,
BEATA MEA, faring far—alone
And weariful—by wistful ways of sleep.
So moved the normal ministry. But great
And singular were interposed events
Which raised it rarely from those faded grooves
About the spurs of which grey characters
Spelt failure. Issues into other paths
Brought other service, now of dying men,
Stricken by hedges, under trees, in wastes
Of perilous rocks. A scowling sun perchance
Through tempest glared, or an attenuate moon
Whiten'd the mournful spaces. In such hours,
Such places, raising the maim'd presences
On her own knees, she gave of that she bare,
Helping the perishing through to further bourne,
Restoring seldom or to life of earth
In dream-life leading back. So also glades
Gave up thatch'd cottages, sequester'd huts,
Where bread was life to mother or to maid
And child in arms. A nimbus moved about
BEATA'S head in ministry like this—
And hers an angel's visits.
      The white Bread
Fail'd not within the Pyx; but whence it came
She wot not; how such mournful service fell

THE QUEST OF A PERFECT SLEEP

Upon her, or the meaning and the end—
These things were veil'd. Beginning there was none,
Through all her life of dream—nothing but this:
The immemorial spaces of sleep's mind
Held nought beside; and well, it seem'd, might one
Who found no vestige in the furthest past
Of starting forth come never unto term—
God's pilgrim ever, through an age before,
An endless age behind.
                        Did God impose
Indeed? A certain vestige of His will
Seem'd in the tying of that inward yoke,
Which thus constrain'd, and would have made it light
Had ever dawn of purpose lifted up
Close-brooding clouds of doubt. Her heart therein
Wearied, if not perchance the psychic limbs.
She pass'd a shadow, dream by dream inwoven,
A presence of beauty, sadness in the soul
Chief immanence within, fell want without,
For all the nations in that shadow'd world
Were starved about her. Darkly shrouded end,
Not less perchance all brightness, shall your sun,
Beyond the vision, soaring upward, still
Long questioning with perfect answer? How
Interpret else that feeling—formless, vague—
Which dwelt within the pilgrim, parted far

From any stage of certitude, and yet
Suggesting not alone a term of quest
But meaning in the whole to compass path
And origin? Would this be found in dream
Or waking? Question for the heart which reads
BEATA'S story, yet beyond her own
Measures of sleep, unknown as dream by her.
Though otherwhere a diverse part of life
Was surely hers, its images were dim:
While shapes of sleep upon the waking state
Broke in, this other—for the conscious soul—
Sank deeper down.
                    Now, while her world of dream
BEATA travels, a phantom bearing bread,
God keep the paths of action and God lead
Through paths of vision to a goal of peace.

I SEE Thy morning brighten;
　Its floods of splendour spread:
O gold beyond the purple
　　And green above the red.
All locks and gates flung backward,
　　Behind the radiant tide
Thy towers and courts are looming,
　　The entrance ways look wide.
When words well'd up within me,
　　As one to witness bidden,
My voice declared Thy presence—
　　Within the cosmos hidden.
Now in the godly coming
　　Of this most gracious day,
Thy rumours throng the threshold
　　And not the far away.
In the blessed now and here
Do I behold Thee near;
And if my earthly seeing
Still veils Thy holy being,
Till other eyes are given,
Of Thee in golden heaven,
When heart of light is open
　　And paths to Thee spread wide,
Will I bear faithful witness
　　As now at morning-tide.

II

Dream-Nomads

AND QUÆSTOR DEI, Brother of our hearts,
   To whom we also wish the end in God,
   A second pilgrim in the world of dream—
Though each to each unknown—bore Wine therein,
And up and down the wistful ways of sleep
A Blessed Chalice in his hands held up,
Through sleepways dark and light—most sacred gift,
He knew not whence, high sign put forth in sleep,
He knew not why. The fabled alkahest
Might so be pour'd, as from another world
On this—high spirit, potent to renew:
Yet craving was not still'd. As she with Bread,
He—darkly mission'd—minister'd in Wine
To multitudes who drank and were athirst.
She was not quench'd who fed the rest, while he
Went famish'd who bore Wine about the world,
And both knew grief, though less for want of theirs

Than service impotent in normal need
To cruel dearth of many. There were times
When all his office, all events therein
Seem'd moving through a world of images,
Of painted signs which signified in vain
For lack of life within him. Could he reach
The hidden meaning, life imparted then
Might make in very truth the wine he bore
A saving gift. In grace of other hours—
Rare visitants, as if from far away—
He felt that something waited to declare
Itself, the term exhibit and perchance
Put end to pilgrim life, from other souls
Apart
          Two nomads of a realm wherein
They moved like living symbols, their dream-world
Itself a show which shows, divided each
From each, observe among the things they shared
In common, one enduring miracle:
The Bread and Wine between them borne and served
Were never wanting. Some unstinted spring
Renew'd the red juice of the mystic grape
In holy Chalice, as in holy Pyx
Was Bread renew'd. Most surely from one source
Of hidden power or grace in the unseen

Both came. Now, what shall follow if they be
Foremeant to meet at one or other point—
The man and maid? When Wine and Bread shall mix,
Will those who want in any place of dream
Be fill'd and satisfied? Will clouded term
Strip off its shadows and will eager eyes
Be lighted up with Knowledge?

                              Keep them, Lord,
Of secret ways and open. Stand about
The pilgrim-hearts who do Thy strange behests,
Till now uncertain that they come from Thee,
But yet with something of good will, towards Thine
Directed. Present in Thy Wine and Bread
Be Thou, the immanence in all, the life
And meaning. Lo, Thy sacraments abide
In all our paths and grace through them flows in;
Meet for the measures of our daily needs,
Our powers of true perception. Most of all
We have tried and proved Thy sacro-saintly food,
And unto some a saving door to Thee
Has open'd there. Beyond these ministries
Of Thine, all doors beyond, we look for Thee.
In waking life we hold within our hearts
Thy dream, and after Thee we strive in sleep:
Through dreams and waking aid, to reach our goal.

TILL I can bless with fingers touch'd by Thee,
    Bless Thou my Bread,
   And bless the Wine by which I look to be
  Through Thine all-ministering bounty fed.
    In all my ways through earthly days
May food of earth become the food of soul
   And food of souls sustain this earthly frame:
      So under one control
Of sacramental law shall earth and heaven
     Become the same.
    For both one food is given,
      And in Thy Name
For these Thy gifts I praise Thee. But if this
   I can and dare, Thy gifts are less than Thou:
    Send down Thy saving grace. Make sacred now
These hands, O Heart of Hallows, nor alone
   For self in blessing; but that Food which is
My life of soul to others let me give,
    That they may also live.
Thy valid consecrations by my own
Be in the shadow-types of words foreshown;
And Thou who art the Giver and the Gift,
    To those who hearts uplift,
    Be Thou made known.

III

A Daughter of Life

BEATA MEA, in the world of men
    Was Eva, shorten'd from Evangeline,
As if she bore unspell'd—in hidden life—
Some gospel-message, on a day beyond,
Predestined to awaken in the heart
And well to lips. The maid meanwhile was fair:
Her beauty brought good tidings to a few.
What else I know not, in the morn of youth,
She gave, except an inward shining sense
And virtue of her clean simplicity.
A little, none too plainly, set apart
By orchid-whiteness of her womanhood
Or one great longing—of the soul to learn
And the soul's end—she went about her ways,
The tasks allotted in her father's house.
Still ways, light tasks, made little call at best
On sources seal'd, capacities within,

To whose own hidden wants that house held none
For ministry—no mother to discern
The roots of need. Her father—kind in heart
Of meaning—dwelt absorb'd, a learned man,
Maker of learned books and known to fame.
By indecisive movements, passing through
His ring-fenced province of material mind,
He felt her famine, but the soul was dream
And the soul's hope for him. Of that and this
He spoke, as one who takes within his thought
A bare, remote hypothesis and turns
One fact about another, to survey
With reason's eye. Detach'd, no light he found,
No life of true concern to that domain
He brought, but wish'd the daughter whom he prized
In his abstracted way might find ere long
Something of life's realities, perhaps
In wedlock, motherhood, the natural cares
Which cast out vague imaginings. What help
Here for a hungry heart, no stir in his
Towards ghostly aims? Distresses and regrets,
Love even, for his one and lonely girl—
If duly weigh'd—were of a kindly heart,
A little puzzled, and far down amused
A little, but live heart—the letter'd man
Had none to prompt within him. It was well
And pleasant when in too brief hours of ease

A DAUGHTER OF LIFE

She sat, low-stool'd, beside him, shaded light
Casting its lustre, gold among the red
Of the rich auburn hair; while glowing hearth
Flush'd the fair face with more than normal warmth
Of changing colour. And though no strict sense
Of definite possession, outside his range—
Second to none—of keen, unfruitful thought,
Kept him in actual touch with things without,
There was a mode, quite tacitly implied,
Wherein the notion of her daughterhood,
Of him as father, interlinking both,
Was counted good, however unexpress'd.

So with this slight, yet serviceable bond
They dwelt together and no burden knew
Therein. The void beneath it and the sad
Awareness that she look'd for help in vain
To him, so quietly assumed by her,
So held as granted, these—in mildness kept—
Took on no deep complexion of distress.
Indeed the want and waiting were themselves
As much her natural, foregranted state
As that strange mission in the place of dream,
Accounted always in the waking ways
A something sacred, haunted and remote,
Not to be shared with any.

                              The clouded term—
By which suspended purpose left the heart
Emptied therein—gave answer from afar
To the world-ways of her, for us who see
That twofold state of life, but not for her,
Or scarcely. There was lonely doom in both,
An arrestation and a formless blank,
The task of doing and of going on,
Truly a task imposed she knew not why.
Poor patience proved in each her main support:
And expectation also, whether more
In sleep or waking she could hardly tell,
Nor I convey. That something, near or far,
Upheld a torch of knowledge in the path
She felt, and so kept on. All these things shaped
Her moods and harbour'd certitude—in both
Her inward states—of being kept apart.
Reflected ever in the waking ways,
That undetermined mission of her dreams
Shut off, she knowing there was none like her
In all her circle. She had talk'd of sleep,
Its mystery, of things that came therein,
And with a certain sacred subtlety
Had sought in others for a whisper'd hint
Of kindred happenings, of work and quest,
But follow'd vainly. There were dreamers round
About her, but of strange continuance

In vision, meaningful or dark like her,
None; and the baffled essay, coupled too
With disconcerting questions in return
On why and what, her own experience—
If any—stifled an experiment
Which jeopardized the secret still her own
And not another's, to be shared at will.

So as in all things else, herein she took
The waiting counsel, spelling to herself
Patience. The word was written in her heart:
Patience, not only for the end of quest,
For hidden purpose shaping things within,
For higher knowledge in the normal mind,
But more for that which wore no certain form,
Though all bespoke its presence—need of love.
So 'twixt desire of light and that profound
Necessity of nature which engulfs
Our being—in possession and absence both—
She stood suspended. Now the viewless term
Shaped itself vaguely as of Things Divine
Encompass'd, now as love uplifting life
And glorifying outward things, in truth
A shining towards her from the shrouded end.

But since self-knowledge, not indeed explored,
Though vistas open'd, shew'd her human love

Asleep within her, stirring in the sleep
And moaning, as if this also dream'd and wept
Frustrated, these twin aspects of the one
Great good, which is all life and earth and heaven,
Work'd in and out and round upon themselves,
Until—reversed in dealings of the mind—
She seem'd to seek the one as if in terms
And symbols of the other, yet attain'd
Neither, so close and yet so far was man,
Though yearn'd for only in the sense of God
Encompassing, indwelling, while how past
All seeing, utterly remote of all
Was all of God.
                      There is but one thing more
To close these plain memorials of a maid
In outward ways, before her change began.
The Churches drew her and the Mass therein;
But records in the hand have fail'd to show
When and how often, if indeed at all—
Except in spirit—she received the Food
Of Souls at earthly Altars. It is known
That something mostly hinder'd—as in dream
She who fed others never broke the bread
She bore in Pyx, because her office served
Not to herself but others. Here on earth,
I think, her unfill'd multitudes of sleep

Spelt a regarded lesson, or some fear
Restrain'd her, lest the indrawn thought of Christ—
The Mystical—should suffer from a rite
Perform'd with partial knowledge, the Bread here
Want life beyond the element and Wine
Reserve the spirit in its shining veil,
A cover'd mystery. But she made at will,
And often, spiritual communions, cast
In spirit—worshipping—on altar steps,
While kneeling bodily in nave or aisle,
Or reservation chapels seal'd with peace
And still'd with sanctity. From far away—
Distance and greatest distance—to the soul
That long'd—she almost saw the end of quest
And almost tasted spiritual food
Of sweetness, while the palpitating chant
Of great invoking litanies inwrapt
Her psychic nature. So at times she lost
The lame unmeaningness of days and dreams,
And on the threshold of a living land
Paused love-inspired. *O Bona Domini,*
Terra viventium. Then the waste itself
Of ill-spell'd dreams and days changed over, took
The grade of life, uplifted in the Breath
Of Life and Spirit—*Terra Exilii,*
Yet also *Bona Domini.*

                        So much
The blessed spirit of the quest on earth,
Uplifted to the holy path of heaven,
Gives me to certify of thy life-steps,
BEATA MEA.

A LITTLE while, a little while,
    Thou hast placed me—a pilgrim here—
    But at first I knew not why,
   Because of the heart's idolatry,
Its making of idols, its worshipping.
   And yet in the hush of the heart I heard,
   Low breathed for ever, one secret word.

A little while, a little while—
   Is it long from cloud to clear?—
    Then out of the dark and its deeps indrawn
    A glimmer, a gleam and a golden dawn
High promise of beauty bring.
   From idols fallen and altar broken
   I turn'd because of Thy secret token.
A little while, a little while,
   Thou wilt gather me hence and steer
    Through ways more open, through ways more fair,
    Ways that are Thine in the otherwhere,
When the soul its flight shall wing.
   But that which is secret, that which is mine,
    In the heart of the soul carry I.
      It is Thine, it is mine;
      It is mine because it is Thine:
   O mystery, meaning and reason why.

IV

A Way in the Waking World

AND the man whose part—
    Unmark'd by each—made answer to her own
    Thus closely in a common mystery:
What of his outer ways? He kept, I know,
Some glimpse of dream-beginnings, or at least
His soul-state pass'd into the waking life,
A sudden dawn of knowledge, on a day
Remember'd well. Behind it spread the time
When conscious life no beacon cast thereon.
But that which fix'd the sovereign fact in mind
Mark'd not an origin in pregnant dream:
As yesterday therein led on to-day
And spoke of morrows, so the past might be
Drawn out unbroken. Leaving clear in thought
No hint of limitation at one end
Or other, possibly pre-natal states

Held that same theme, and life past earth perchance
No other: so did his experience
Repeat BEATA'S. But this blank of blanks
Reacted ever in the outward ways
Diversely on an eager, restless heart,
Quick with desire, as sudden in resolve,
All ready to rebel but not to wait—
Saving the soul in patience. Hence his name
Of QUÆSTOR DEI, for his life in verse
As fitting symbol chosen. Not to hide
That which counts nothing, poor identity
On earth, it reaches over to express
A sacramental nature, up and down
Strange ways of thought and effort urging fast
And moiling. There turn'd back, it broke up here
Whatever barr'd; or at an alley's end
Finding no better than a wall's sheer height—
Past scaling—yet unconquer'd, once again
It veer'd and so restarted. Labour wins
Result at last; the crown descends thereto,
And high desire—upleaping and aflame—
Soars to attain it.
                    Now, the sleepless heart
Of QUÆSTOR DEI toil'd after truth and God.
Resolve was ever towards the end; misease
At let and hindrance was the chafe at self

And its preventing chain. Rebellion too
Withstood no idle postulate of doom
Or God's opposing will, but failing worth
To follow on a call so high, but weak
And errant nature, all within the man
Which miss'd the goal conceived. These, in his thoughts,
Kept back, these made the warfare of his world
Faint-hearted tactics, he so prone to yield,
Call truce, so tempted towards a shameful peace.
Perchance misdoubt and such reproach made up
The bar erected. In his heart he knew
The quest was follow'd, being part of growth,
And to forestall was foolish in the hope,
Nor came to aught, save new impediment.

So also moods befell, when unawares
The contest ceased: a little while the soul
Reposed as on the open hand of God,
Resign'd and temper'd. Then the strange dreamlife
Display'd its miracle of guidance; then
Expectant mind foresaw what lay beyond—
Not in clear vision, yet from doubt set free—
As some fair end in knowledge and in light.
Then also QUÆSTOR DEI felt and knew
What place apart he held. He did not need
To sift acquaintance, so to stand assured

That no man slept himself into a world
Like his. That it must take him in good time
To some unwitted term—here faith came in;
The high sincerity and truth of God
Involved this and assured. But more than all
He knew dream-life into the waking life
Had brought salvation, brought the note of quest,
Made known that something somewhere in the world
Was waiting, not beyond a strenuous search
And not so much desirable or fair
As very need, meaning and life of being.

For the rest, QUÆSTOR DEI stood unyoked,
Without possessions or prosperity,
Without adversity, or pinch of want,
In a middle and moderate way, some daily bread
Earn'd, nor too hardly—how shall matter not.
Poet he was by virtue of the gift,
Not quite unheeded. A young, earnest man
And student, clean of thought and in his life
Clean, he resolved on God and his own soul's
Unfoldment, rather as a work in God
Than as demanding guerdon, not in fear
Of loss, yet anxious lest he miss the term
And go in darkness who should walk in light.

His past knew other searchings, but the dream

Had saved him, dawning into consciousness;
Had once conceived unutterable loss
And found it dwell within him. In his verse
He pictured one who took such loss to heart
As pre-elected to its nameless charge—
For the whole world's salvation. When this theme
Grew first within him, when from more to more
He shaped it, zealous and absorb'd therein,
The thing possess'd him, the thing lived in him—
Subject and self inwoven and inbound.

The more he dwelt upon that darksome tale,
Touch'd and retouch'd the record, not to gild,
Not to adorn with picture-light of words,
But there and here to give the guise of truth
And very seeming, the more it work'd in him,
On him laid hold. A sickness of the mind
Came over him: the imaged life became
His own. In stresses of a final draft,
A last sad conquest in reality,
It seem'd that something which was more than self
Empower'd him to accept the part of doom.
That which his mind had fashion'd and evolved
Cross'd the dim threshold between art and life,
Lodged after as a madness in the brain,
And haunted. Exorcizing power of will
Was baffled. Panic follow'd, then the time

Of a still frenzy, as he took the dread
Into his heart and nursed it, help'd the growth
Within, consented and was crucified.

The grand climacteric of a single night
Wrote itself—a red fire—in heart and head.
He rent the poem and its fragments knew
Another flame. His witness was himself,
All else flash'd back false seeming, having cast
Self beyond hope apart. To satisfy
Such woe with record were some weak attempt
To comfort that which neither man nor God
Would rest henceforth. But then, another mood:
So great a tragedy of all the worlds
Might well be burnt into a few brief lines,
That man at least might know. And so he wrote,
As one whose stylus in the darkness halts,
Whose hand shakes, shaping an uncertain word,
Or misspells half his message in the night:
Night all, both word and thought, most dreadful night;
And in the soul that dark on which no dawn
Was look'd to break, world without end prolong'd.

I KNOW that life is Thine and life is Thou,
   That life is life, O Lord, for evermore:
  Thou the beginning and Thou the end and Thou
    The after and before—
That which abides betwixt the here and now,
    And there and then.
But death is that which stands from Thee apart
In empty nothingness eternally;
    For Thou art all. Amen.
A Life in life, where'er I move Thou art,
And growth is mine in Thee from more to more:
   Shall aught of soul to naught of death respond?
I am alive in Thee and cannot die,
But pass from star to star, from shore to shore,
   In vast of this world and more vast beyond,
Imploring knowledge of my soul in Thee,
   Its deeps to penetrate, its heights endow:
     Knowledge of Thee in me,
     Till Thine in Thee is Thou.

V

A Tale of Eternal Death

"THE saviour of the unborn worlds to come"—
    So shaped his story of eternal death—
    "Renouncing type and parable, speaks once
And there is henceforth no more prophecy.

"I pledged myself to seek diviner life,
Flinging the past behind; with stedfast face,
Look'd forth on truth; and one of all the world
Dared all the heights. Not so the mission came.
Heights fail'd: upstanding as on peaks of thought,
Meseem'd the mazes of the mind enwound
Still, and beyond them was unpeopled void—
God hidden in the spaces 'twixt the stars
And more in solar glory deeply veil'd.
But thought, the darkest curtain, hung between
Heart and essential being. Self likewise
Barr'd self from knowledge, open'd gulfs between

Man and that great unmanifest Divine
Deep-seal'd within him. Paralysed I fell
To night and nothing. In my darkness then—
Helpless and humbled—the dread mission came.
It gave me darkness for my place, and hope
My broken lamp—all purpose miss'd but one.
As Christ flung back Heaven's gates to all who came
Believing and embracing, so could I
Shut up the gates of hell by passing through
And there abiding, through a work of will,
Not slave's compulsion. Mine free choice of heart,
And choice alone could make the mission mine.
I testify as one who knelt and pray'd,
In blacker garden than Gethsemane,
For cup more bitter than was drunk of old
By Mount of Olives to be taken hence.
That cup still offer'd unto shrinking lips,
Nor was mine angel mission'd to console.
In fine I drank it to the dregs, all pain,
All wrath accepting in the inmost self,
That I might bring thee, World, from doom and woe.
Body and soul into the gulf I cast,
And fill it: now thou canst not fall therein.
Hell's House is shut against thee by these hands,
While from the dolorous place, all hope beyond,
I peer between the bars, and thee so fair,

Redeem'd unwittingly, my World, I see.
Account it thou the chiefest test of love
That though no Word Divine has come to mark
Such sacrifice as ratified above—
The mission only from the mind itself
Unfolded, self-conceived, self-built and last
Self-taken—I hold God's silence like a word
Of doom-encompassing consent; and that
Accorded, utter dereliction now
Descends and certifies the offering.
I cry not—woe is me—with God's strong Son
That 'Why hast Thou forsaken me?'—which seal'd
His mission and reveal'd Divinity.
My passion and the long-drawn life thereof
Seems more than Golgotha or Calvary,
For consciousness of Godhead unobscured
Supported Him; but I am man alone:
Nor special strength has nerved, nor man has dream'd,
Nor Nature known.
                              "Here in this testament
The inspiration which inform'd me once
At length bereaves me. Now my voice has lost
Its early ring; the lightness from this pen
Has vanish'd: there is lead in every line.
Without conviction in the weight it drags,
By every word I wrong the cause I own,

And my poor life which, from this garrulous state
Apart, might take some touch of the sublime—
Because it was so secret and so still—
Counts itself out in folly at the end.

"Yet must I speak: so only man shall know
That one unaided, voluntary act
Has taken to my heart the whole world's shame,
Even the unrepented yoke thereof,
For evermore. Who deems I err herein?
Nay, God in fine is mercy and would send
Some envoy surely of his hierarch-host
To turn my path, if I deceived myself—
To scourge me, were I blinded with my pride.
The unassisted agony wherein
This soul must keep shall over quickly quench
All shining spectacles of sacrifice;
Yet should I madden past the second death—
World—could I save thee not. And Thou, O Lord,
Make this self-ruin grateful in Thy sight,
But do not let one wrathful shaft of flame,
From Thine eyes scorch, but for a moment's space,
One fibre of man's being.
     "Man, forgive
This unskill'd harping on the creaking strings
Of my worn thought. Behold, I pass through life
Anonymous, unknown, who might have seal'd

Such mission with a gorgeous ministry,
Sending apostles and disciples forth
Through all the world, to conquer every heart,
To bid them cease from evil and so make
My stripes perchance the fewer. Through pleasant paths
Of rose-leaf creed, for all in truth but one,
Hereafter, haply I had led the earth
To temple me, so taking full delight
Of pomp and splendour from the peak of doom,
Self-poised o'er all in god-pre-eminence.
I might have met Diana the divine—
High love—upon a golden night of nights—
Yea, on some marriage-night of main and sky—
And in a silent, passion-haunted place,
On which the stars shed influence benign,
Where stars and moon concur, have known her grand
And holy secret. So for this, for all
Foregone, acquit me when my weakness calls
On distant pulse of love from those I love
To travel towards me through the sable voids.
Trust me, in fine, to hold thee freed. Spare all
Thou canst of all that hurts me. On my part
I do repent me not. With heart aflame,
Here I renew, a meek but stedfast man,
My godly sacrifice.
              "Refulgent light

Bared in the stormy West—fire-fill'd abyss—
A conscious life assume and hear my pledge."

So broke the testament, reaching a kind of close
In frenzy. Ave, Poet. He became
His own dread epic; lived it out in heart;
Took back, accepted; and again took back.
So crazing more and more, he spilt himself
Towards death or madness, then was sick to death,
But at the end, by mercy, fell in strange,
Far-haunted sleep. The mission-life of dream
Broke there upon him, an old tale maybe,
Long since rehearsed; but coming back with him
For the first time into his waking world,
That other dream which long distracted life
Led forth its darksome pageant and went down
Below the mind's horizon.   So it was
With QUÆSTOR DEI, bearing Cup of Dream,
When something flowing over life of earth
Brought on salvation.

I AWOKE in Thy sunlight,
   I lived in Thy light:
  Very good, very sweet has it been,
For all I have heard and seen
  Has been songs and visions of Thee.
In the golden haze or the noon-white blaze
And the violet height of the brooding night
    Were images—all of Thee.
I have found Thee, Master of life and Lord:
  In all true voices Thy voice alone,
    And written on star and stone
    Thy sigils of act and word.

May I, who awaken'd to hear and see
The sounds so bless'd and the sights of Thee,
Pass off at length into states more deep,
The finding and keeping of perfect sleep,
    And awaken after in Thee.

VI

The House of Many Mansions

A HOUSE of Many Mansions, lifted up,
   Arch over arch, wall above wall, with towers
   And spires, its portals soaring towards the sky—
An unimaginable vastness—fill'd
The open space, wherein the woodland path
Ceased suddenly. A mist was on the wold
Woven about BEATA, gazing still'd.
A blotted moon, distended in the mist,
Sifted the pallid vapours and infused
A swooning light. The stedfast ways of sleep
Had brought her up all suddenly, unwarn'd,
Against that admirable pile. Between
The parted hedge she look'd, as one transfix'd,
Across the saturated mead's great stretch
And at that mighty vision straight in front,
Keeping the whole horizon. So might one

Stand startled, stricken, unaccountable,
To some strange star all suddenly transferr'd.
It was a very silent place—Amen—
In a silent world. Whatever breeze or wind
Lived, in the breathing hush'd, had fallen low
And, if it moved, stirr'd stilly wavering.
Whatever life abode in leaf or blade
Was being suspended. In BEATA died
Heart and heart's rhythm. A cold fear at first
Slipp'd through her veins of being. But this pass'd
In wonder, reaching out from its own state
To that of worship. Hence as one in prayer
Clasps hands, to interlock the sense of God,
She raised her Pyx to grasp the sense of height.
And round about that unchased silver vase
The moonlight fell and whiten'd. So stood she,
By grades grown conscious in the secret soul
That—long days over, the rogation weeks
Past—her uncertain and uncounted months,
Telling off years, had attain'd at length
Their whole duration's culminating point,
Till now there loom'd a threshold of the end,
And there should presently be no more veils
But high, intelligible purpose, glass'd
In the great term attain'd.
                              A patient ghost
Among ghost-dwellers, from a land of ghost

THE HOUSE OF MANY MANSIONS

Emerging, all that lay behind her steps—
Of places and durations—seem'd about
To take on vestures of reality,
While she towards something vibrant in the heights
And deeps of being, to the truth and life
Of things moved surely. Now—no longer ghost
Or body of fleshly life, but soul awake—
Or swiftly passing towards the waking state—
She with uplifted arms and bended head,
Crossing the meadow spaces, paused again,
Those roofs and towers above her. That which came—
Here in the closer presence of the House—
Was neither sense of peace welling within
Nor sense-possessing majesty of span
From base to summit, but the measureless,
The abounding possibility of all
In and outside relation to herself.

Of how the great end should its scope affirm,
Or where she was, no intimation came,
Nor conscious need thereof. Unguerdon'd toil,
Lone ways, unprofitable moods of thought
Were over—this, for ever. Was she meant
To cross those precincts ? Was it holy ground
Within ? Such questions did not leave her mind
Uncertain. Would the mighty doors move back
Unbidden, to admit her, or she wait—

A silent, watchful postulant—through days
Or moons her summons? Nay, in a good hour
She came, and this was the appointed place.
That which had brought her to a pause without
Look'd now pure worship of a heart set free;
And worshipping she moved, from step to step
Ascending. Then upon the last, with head
Still bow'd, the vessel in her hands upraised,
In the white flickering of the moon, she pass'd
Within. But whether through an open'd door
Or as pure spirits glide, finding no bar,
Which of us seeks to know, and who shall say?

Behold BEATA MEA in the House
Of Many Mansions, now received in dream;
And the good God, Who takes some souls in sleep
But some in waking to their term in Him,
Give her good issue out of dreams and all
Which counts with us for waking, that true life
And its most high fruition be hers in Him.

I know not, ask not, through what halls or aisles
Her heart's dream-images had drawn the maid:
Were such my own adventure, beyond doubt,
The sacraments of sleep would have been clothed
In other vestures: unto each his dream
And unto each its pageantry. But she

THE HOUSE OF MANY MANSIONS

In chantry or in chapel, transept, nave—
It matters little—at due time attain'd
That which was given to be reached, and so
A valid moral to the quest of sleep.
Altar or Table—was it that or this?—
She stood enwrapp'd on one or other side
And waited: the oblation of white Bread
Within the Pyx seem'd light upon the hands
Which held. A hush'd expectancy possess'd
Her being, without haste and without search
Tarrying awhile in very certainty,
While in the stillness came a very sense
Of God's most utter wholeness—nothing slipp'd
Apart or wanting. All her thought within
Sank gently down into a calm, deep pool
Of pure mind-being, from vicissitude
And chequer of complexion perfectly
Deliver'd—into an embracing state
Of uttermost awareness. So abide,
BEATA, Altar and Ciborium
Have left awhile no image in your heart,
And there is nothing but the formless, free
Unmodal certitude of God in all.

What space of time unmeasured in her dream
Elapsed, I know not. On such side of life
That mute duration drawn within the self

Was like a contemplation in the heart—
Unbiass'd by the mark of hours or days.
But, still inwoven, at a certain point
It grew within her that the vaulted place
Encompassing was vastness in the vast
Of halls and chambers. That which fronted her
Show'd endless in the shadows, and the moon
Through some interminable window shone
Behind her, utterly remote. Thereat
Her lifted eyes look'd forward, placid-like,
Aware that having been alone, and long
Within the measures of her single self,
Such tide of circumstance was breaking here
A last wave on the bourne. From what far end
She knew not, growing into human shape,
There came a figure which, with shining eyes,
Held mute communion—not less deep than hers—
In his own being. Betwixt hands he bore
A Chalice and drew on as one who moves
But does not walk. The altar's further side
Reaching, he paused. Thus did the man and maid
Confront each other; so the Pyx and Cup
Were met together in a Holy Place:
So QUÆSTOR DEI and BEATA join'd
Their life in dream.
      Another door than hers
Received him; by another path he drew

Within that House of Souls. The world of sleep
Which him enfolded on the self-same night
Had shown him hills encompassing, a steep
And rocky way beneath a blending moon;
And he went down, somewhat as one who toils,
Proceeding slowly—not as yet indeed
Conscious of end, yet hearing in the heart
An unvoiced witness that the mode of dream
Led on to that of vision. In the hope
Hereof, he fared among the hills and crags,
Until at length they stood on either side
Behind him, while in front the mystic House—
Vision indeed—loom'd suddenly across—
It might be—glebe-land in a great expanse.
Now, on this side of it the moon was clear
And the high mastery of the mighty pile
Stood forth, sharp-angled towards the base and lost,
If lost indeed, as spires and pinnacles
Melting in yellow light, with all the depth
Shut off in continuity sublime
Behind.
      Hereat the mission'd seeker knew
There came his first great moment of the quest,
And his essential being leap'd within,
As child in womb outreaching into birth.
Thereafter, born into that world unknown,
He cross'd the threshold, Thus, with open eyes

But soul indrawn, at once most surely led
And self-directing, worshipful, he pass'd
High precincts, oriels and vaulted rooms,
An altar reaching at the end, and saw—
Beneath moon-litten window—that white maid
Hidden in contemplation and moon-veil
Of unshaped nimbus.
                      Whether spoken word
Or thought's communion follow'd meeting eyes
Shall matter not. The terms we use on earth
Are sacraments of interchanging souls
And thus we know each other—but in part,
With bars between. If speech seems used in sleep,
Perchance so only to our waking hours
Can recollection in the soul convey
Her messages from spiritual mind
Through the material brain. Hence all is clothed
In symbols—thought and love. The modes of speech
Are emblematic, like the arms' embrace
And the entrancing meeting of the lips.
Only in each and all we prove at times
What unplumb'd wells remain—the unexpress'd
Within—what fountains and what fires leap up
Towards manifestation, but to fail therein.
And then we know, beyond our space and time,
Past shapes and ways of thought or loving act,
We also, grafted on reality,

Draw roots of being from the eternal world
And flow through all things.
                            She who sank therein
And for the first time found her nature's deeps—
BEATA MEA—to the psychic state
Returning slowly, and he—less withdrawn
But rather vigilant in both his worlds
For living vision as a crown of dreams—
Saw in the half-light each the eyes of each
Resplendent, growing from the human mode
To high-uplifted spiritual states
Wherein the God-ray from the centre pours
Through every bond of being. There and then—
As those who reach a place for rest ordain'd
And find that Eden's bowers are not beyond
The hammer'd pathways of a weary world,
Or those who seek a hostel of the Lord
Through convent-gate and reach a mercy-seat
Shelter'd by wings of cherubim—with one
Accord they set the Chalice down and Pyx.
Then with cross'd arms and interlinking hands
They gave the watchwords of that secret hour
Through inward reading eyes, perchance in speech,
But most by sudden union of the soul,
Far from all jar and shock, as quiet streams
Converge and mingle, where the water-ways
Meet on a level ground.

How many Houses in Thy Name are builded
   And in the shadow of Thy presence dwell,
By aspiration raised, while faith has welded
   The holy stones with craft of holy spell.
But there is one behind them or above
   Which is not built of hands or heart of man,
Great Architect thereof Eternal Love,
   Who built in wisdom ere the world began.
From this the soul comes forth, to this returns:
   About it shines the Presence which is He;
Abiding Glory in the chancel burns
   And blessed hierarchies their Master see.
But past the chancel, past the Holy Place,
   As in an All-God dark of dread abyss,
A plenitude of being and of grace,
   Lies that most hidden centre which is His.
No forms emerge therefrom, no forms go in,
   But that which is not mode in me and you,
An inmost root of being, dwells therein,
   Gulf-deep, beyond the viewing and the view.
Now this is that from which we are, and by
   This does our endless to the endless cleave,
Our spaceless with the unspaced unify.
   Seek, and all separating worlds retrieve:
Beyond the silence and beyond the speech,
Seek inward, soul of mine and soul of each.

VII

A Dream in the Quest of God

THE lonely ways
   Of long dream-life slipp'd from them silently.
The spacious presages of things to come
Spread vistas widely, peopled far and near
With cohorts of prevision, angel-hosts
Thronging a court of heaven. When something loosed
All bounds and bonds, they stood as those on whom
The kingship of the spiritual city
Confers its freedom. In such hour the soul
Enlarged its auras, and that moon which look'd
From her far height upon them, with its beams,
Form'd pallid background where each shone to each
In radiant light of beauty. They beheld
Enough of coming things to know that God
And the Divine Ambassadors keep well

The future ways, shaping them all in love
To perfect ends. Moreover, in the glass—
Clear and bright-shining—of each other's eyes
They look'd and saw some part of that which lay
Behind in their unfathom'd past of things.
Not here and now their primal meeting-point,
Nor in the sleep of far anterior worlds,
Or waking life in elder days of earth,
But in the spirit they had dwelt with God—
Beyond distinctions of the twain and Him—
Together, He alone possessing all
And all in Him: unsearchable unity,
Infinite multiplicity.
                So came
The gospel of their eyes and spoke itself
Within their hearts, preach'd from the soul of both,
Received and realized in heart and soul.
The dream had grown to vision: if in sleep,
It was a sleep in God. The eyes of her
Were gates for an expanding universe,
And the whole world was she, desired in God,
In God received—a blessed sacrament,
Image and type of Him. On her own part
BEATA'S wells of being leap'd, and she
Saw God alone in eyes through which she look'd,
God in the cosmic vistas far prolong'd
Beyond their gate, an unescapable,

All-keeping love. And she herself became
No longer loving or of things beloved
But love itself, with God of God therein.

Thus were they open'd and replenish'd thus
Within them. Each to one another given
Forecast not then concerning future lots
And waking life together. They inwove
At root, in essence, knowing that the bond
Was not in holy house or place of dream
Welded, but that which had for ever been,
Though only now discover'd. Being fill'd
Themselves, they also saw the end of want
Among the famish'd peoples of their sleep.
So therefore in the Blessed and Holy House
Of Many Mansions, inly moved thereto,
And in a silence both of lips and heart,
They seal'd refreshment and its grace attain'd,
Communicating each to each the Bread
And Wine, so long in separation borne,
But now in union shared. A secret wealth
Hidden in that communion raised for them
Some further gates, sluice-gates of very light,
As if through channels of the outward signs
The life and substance of God's hidden deeps
Flow'd in them and flow'd over and immersed—
A saturation of the Soul with God.

One moment only they were drown'd therein,
And all the canticles of saints and Kings,
Whom God has visited in fullness, join'd
In clamorous melody. It was good to dwell
In the Lord's House, the beauty of that House
O'er all desired; to stand within the gates
Of this true Zion; to sing with golden tongue
The mystery of eternal life in Him,
As blood and body received in body and blood.
They look'd towards that great day when all who strive
In their poor hearts for God and Things Divine
Shall feel their hearts a cellarage of God
Press'd down, fill'd over, pouring through the streets
Of spiritual cities; the worldly rich
Left empty, till they also starve, and God
Shall also them replenish.
                         I have said
One moment—very transport, yet too still
For words of mine. The spirits had dissolved
Together, into God's great dark withdrawn.
But they had far to travel in the soul
And what befell them on one side of life
To reach upon the other. Therefore this
Viaticum of rapture came and went
Flashwise, and never in their life of dream
Did they come bearing Bread and Wine again

To feed each other. At the end of all,
When those who now stand in the Outer Court
Shall cross the Holy Place and after—raised
Towards the Holy of Holies—find the last
Most highest veil, perchance upon their call
Awaiting, they may minister once more
To one another, or the veil itself
Be parted by a ministry behind.
Then God shall draw them through, while other voice
Than theirs recites the *consummatum est*.

Quantum magnale Dei gaudium:
Come, taste and prove the sweetness of the Lord,
Glory of joy in Him, the King Whose joy
Is to be known in hearts, Who else abides
Unknown, received not in the part of life.
Mayst thou, O Word of all, in all take flesh:
Those which conceive Thee in embodied womb
Of soul and bring Thee forth into their lives
Shall make one flesh together, one heart and soul.
Here are true marriages, my spouse, my love—
BEATA MEA. Consummations here
Are perfect for all life, death and beyond—
O QUÆSTOR DEI, spiritual friend,
Most High Companion of the Holy Quest.
So in one night of sacrament those twain

Grew one into another: they were known
And knew. Wide openings of the cryptic way
Were made within them and the vistas shone—
World upon world. At that still rapture's end
They stood together, but now side by side,
Bearing the Chalice and Ciborium
For other needs than theirs. The light within
Was light without, fair-flowing through the House.
The Sacred Presence manifest within
Show'd forth another Presence like thereto—
Nay, but the same and self-declared without,
Through all the hallow'd images and veils,
Though not set wholly free from certain clouds,
As might be incense-fumes from thuribles
Or sanctuary chant down nave and aisles
Panting and pouring, muffling for the most
That still, small voice which in the shrouded Pyx
Recites the blessed privities of God.

So much—towards vision in elected hearts—
Of many mansions in the House of God
And chambers of the Presence.

FOR what from me could hide Thee
    In worlds without I sought
Who needed none beside Thee;
    But there I met with naught.

With golden tongues for leading
    All Nature's glories preach,
And beauty spreads for reading
    Her gospels, clear as speech.

Where earths and skies and seas are,
    The witness never fails:
Thy revelations these are
    And not Thy clouding veils.

I only then conceal Thee:
    Strip off this self, and I
Shall unto That reveal Thee
    Which not in self can die:

A Thou within my being
    Which past all mine and me,
My ways of thought and seeing,
    Is I at one with Thee.

VIII

A Garden of Life

BEATA MEA on the search for God
    And QUÆSTOR DEI on the self-same quest,
In expectation bless'd and looking forth
Beyond their present measures, from the bonds
Of these, towards ends attain'd and fruit thereof:
Learn how it fared with both in waking ways,
After the dreams and visions of the night
Had open'd their new epoch in the life
Of sleep and dual drama of the soul.

She in sunlitten gardens of the house,
Among the peacocks and fantastic trees—
Uncouthly shaped—at the glad morning-tide,
Before the shining city—far below—
Had waken'd fully; he from mesh of streets
Emerging on the brimming river's side,
Between the bridges; ponder'd on the night
And that new gospel of the life of trance

Which both had shared, though each to each unknown
In outward ways. One dream-experience
Therein, so also in the aftermath
One thought was kindled in the mind and one
Burnt in the heart of each—the when and where
Of earthly meeting. Somewhere in the world
She lived in flesh, somewhere he dwelt with men.
No common hunger after human love
Made quick that thought. They had not kiss'd in sleep,
Since deeper ways are open to the soul,
With soul in search of union. Mindful now
Of that which was, no longing in the hearts
Enter'd, but certitude of things to come
Left therewithin a hundred doubts unsolved
On what must follow meeting. Would their ways
Be cast henceforth together? Nay, not this—
Too preassured already. Would those twain
Grow one in waking life? And nay, not that:
No earthly life divides what sleep makes one
When soul in vision is deeply bound with soul.
But wheresoever such foreseen event
Should cross the threshold of their circumstance,
Would those great wells which they had sounded once
Unseal again? Would past and future fling
Gates open to the future and the past?
Would they see farther back and yet more far

Before them in the Mystery of God?
They could not meet within the common bonds
Of strangers: that was certain. Yet perchance
The things within might cast on those without
Pale reflex only, from true life apart
And its unplumb'd reality. Perchance
It must be so, for on the side of sleep
Abode henceforth the very truth of truth,
The constant light of light; but here, like shades
Or aspens, flicker'd on the waking side
All painted images of things without.
At most on this the omens moved and shone,
But there the great moralities. So sign
And signified, in this the aftermath,
Stood parted clearly on confronting banks
Of being.
        Better in his heart he knew
Than haply she that this was mood alone—
And fleeting. Presently the focus lost
Would find itself, the shifted balance turn,
Adjust and compensate. For both no less
The speculation issued and the doubt,
Bearing their saving clauses at the end,
Since—howsoever it might prove at first—
Not on one only side of life there dwells
Reality, and not on one the soul

Attains. The gates would open here as there,
The deeps unseal; and late or soon the twain
Should know each other, as in sleep they knew—
At one, and thus for ever. Granted this
For utter certainty, and passing hence
Unchallenged, there remain'd on either side
A certain failing of the heart in face
Of such foregone encounter, for the how
Of its beginning, for grey common light
Which might encompass, those first banal words
Of greeting, that first obvious wonderment,
For all the limits of mere earthly eyes,
Slow growth in learning one another's ways,
Status, pursuits, diurnal interests.

What if at first those twain, so near in soul
And fill'd with mission when the inward world
Was lifting veils from off its infinite,
Should in the manifest body and life to each
Prove scarcely possible? What if meeting's doom
Came on them at a corner of the streets,
In hurry and drive of rain, draggled and drench'd?
His more than hers this special pictured dread;
But she had pictures. Setting those which bless'd
To cancel those which tortured, she lived down
The spaces of suspense, and he at last
Discharged all images and look'd towards sleep.

But this fail'd both: an utter blank in dream
Had follow'd after that revealing night,
Till they remember'd that the leaves of life
In sleep turn'd slowly, discontinuous,
Though nought seem'd miss'd, while any will of theirs
For nothing counted.

I HAVE lived among the symbols
  Of Thy great dramas long;
The pomp of Thy pontificals
  About me moves in song.

Thine Art sends forth its tidings
  In all the play-scenes round me;
Its grace uplifting Nature
  To her World-Rites has bound me.

Give me High Grades for ever,
  All parts in Thy masques to try,
More and yet more of Thy pageants,
  Their meaning and mastery.

IX

The Master Comes

WHEN a week had pass'd,
    As earthly air of old at times gave up
Some blessed spirit in the guise of man,
Or—when all doors were shut—the risen Christ
Stood in an upper room, invoking peace
On true disciples, so life's native mode
And daily sequence to BEATA gave
One unto her as Master—not that man
Of vision with the chalice in his hands,
Knowing and known in unity. Some two
Or three mere shadows in the life of her—
Met there or here, at lecture or at home—
Brought them together, from design apart,
And something in the white-hair'd, travell'd man
Had drawn her father. So at the right time,
In the right way, by manifest design
Untinged, he came who saw and knew within.
Perhaps with open knowledge of her life

In dream he came: she told him naught thereon.
His silence notwithstanding, something spoke
Within her and bore witness to the heart
That neither waking life nor life of sleep
Were hidden from his inward eyes. She felt
Unveil'd before him who was veil'd to her,
Though not indeed as one who vests himself
In mystery, or willingly shuts fast
The doors of secret spirit or of mind.

He seem'd uplifted in the height of things,
Beyond all common vision, into rest
Of knowledge and possession in the still
And active centre. She had seen the soul
As one who on the threshold of a world
Looks down its vistas. He abode therein
And came not therefore with the types and signs
Of outward sacraments, in bread and wine;
As any spokesman of a church or creed,
Of any system warranted by man;
As bearing seals of mission, set on that
Or this—in high hypothesis—by God.
His the authority of very life,
Which makes no claim, but is and is confess'd.
The fountain-springs of self-hood and its notes
Were missing, and the impression so produced
Was not of one who has effaced the self

THE MASTER COMES

But, in the measures of a wider world
Increased, has come into a higher state,
Another heritage, a cosmic mode.
Being that she was, no special words of his
BEATA needed to communicate
This and things deeper than such terms convey.
His presence and its quality of life
Awaken'd. As the incense in the church
Entrances sense and thus the thurible,
Amidst the blessed fragrance over aisles
And nave, is counted nothing but goes by
Unheeded, so the Master as a man
Of flesh was in the nowhere and the naught
For her, but all—in silence or in speech—
The life-evoking quality of life
Which dwelt about him and for her was he.
Moreover, on his lips our common words
Took on another vesture. Had he talk'd
Pure trifles, idly as an old man might,
Or blended things which pass with things that stay
And matter, lest a woman in her youth,
Just raised from girlhood, find it hard to stand
In thought at full attention, still his words—
To her at least and others tuned like her—
With life vibrating, would have pass'd life on
And with deep modes of music stirr'd deep chords
Of very soul within.

                    A word indeed,
But one sufficed, wherever God's great Name
Was utter'd, for there flash'd through him to her
Light plenary from infinite of things,
As if it had been spoken from the heart
Of Heaven. The path, the end of all her quest
Were voiced therein. She felt the sacrament
Of simple words, and the dry bones of speech
Lived, moved: so utter'd in the depths of her
They traversed all her galleries and crypts.
She answer'd from the soul in sympathy
Of understanding love—at times with lips,
More often in that silence of the mind
Which answers fully through the speaking eyes.
So learn'd she and so grew. He spoke at times
Of Hidden Mysteries in Holy Church.
Then all distinctions between Church and World
Were brought to nothing; there was unity
Of Grace and Nature, being Grace in all;
And this was Nature raised upon the heights
Of holiness. On woman and on man
He spoke, and there was oneness in the depth
And height of consecrate humanity,
Sub specie amoris—so alone—
Regarded: all was kingship and high light
In the great vistas opening before
And round them. It recall'd that vision-state

THE MASTER COMES

When her soul open'd and the soul of him
Who stood upon the farther altar-side,
While far beyond that prefatory state
Lay other worlds of union, here reveal'd
To mind alone. And she remember'd too
That at the close of such high change in sleep—
She knew not how—the altar interposed
No longer; but they, standing side by side,
Prepared upon a predetermined path
To take their course and so perchance exchange
A state of soul far looking into soul
For two in one abiding self-immerged.

Observe, her Master never chose a theme
As one with office to discourse thereon,
Nor ever spoke as teacher. That and this
Of each high subject out of this and that,
Among the seeming accidents of things,
Issued, and self-presented unawares
Became their theme, which heaven-born wisdom's art
Seal'd with great Nature's own simplicity.

Music of words which subtly work'd their spell
Outside all conscious knowledge or intent,
And silence after as at end of song:
I know not which gave most, but both had light
And warmth of teaching for the need she had,

While her responding nature lifted up
And—as a tree of many roses draws
The life-increasing dews—drew springs of speech
Within, or sheen of subtle silences,
As rose from golden sun derives at once
Beauty and nutriment. So too, as this
Gives forth a royal fragrance in return,
She radiated quick with sympathy,
True understanding, answers from the heart.
Thus was there antiphon and fair response
Continually between them, and behind
The outward Church of Nature and of Grace
She pass'd in spirit to the Church within,
And through such incense of the Master's words
Beheld the Blessed Mystery of all
Inward experience taking outward form.
The *Sacramentum ineffabile,*
The Holy Graal upheld by priestly hands
Shone out dilucid over altar height.

But afterwards alone, in worship rapt
And ravish'd, reverent over radiant Cup
Bent the adoring face of him who stood
Before her in the many-mansion'd House,
While she, Pyx-Bearer, held on virgin breast
The great white secret which is Bread of Life.
This aspect ceased. Thereafter, side by side

Standing, the sacred vessels glow'd in light
Together. Then a little while, and then
One vessel only, which was Pyx and Cup,
Till this dissolved, and Christ between them stood
One moment's space. *Valete,* time and life,
All separate sense of being and of thought;
But that which was and is and is to come
Abode alone in them and they therein—
Eternal Life in Christ.
                        But thence return'd
Within the normal measures of our life,
BEATA MEA, by the reasoning mind,
Discern'd in part and very far away
That in some sense to be hereafter known
Her nature answer'd to the Bread she bare
And must be changed into the Bread of Life,
While he—brought strangely into worlds of dream—
Stood in some deep relation to the Cup
He carried and must suffer change himself,
Till that which answer'd to its wine became
The Wine of Life, Blessed and Holy Graal.

THY Word is buried in the heart of man,
    Below the life of sense:
  Of all creation Thou art life and plan,
  The essence and the immanence.
But, ah, for us the hidden Godhead sleeps
  In cosmic Nature and is veiled in ours,
Till something calls it from unsounded deeps
  To rise within us and unfold its powers.
    Then shall great Nature stir
And putting sleep for us away from her
    Shall also wake.
  How shall that morning break?
O not in East or West alone
  And not from here or there:
  At once and everywhere
The Christ Who comes within is seen and known,
  The Voice of Life is heard,
  Life of all life and Word.
O admirable Presence, Voice Divine,
Thy world is ours and mine;
And to Thy light, transfigured, shall respond
In light the worlds without us and beyond.

X

The Way of the Waterside

BEYOND the city, by the South and West,
    Far over fields and meadows, heath and down,
By stream and fell, in recollected thought
Fared QUÆSTOR DEI, at the quiet end
Of this same week wherein the dream of sleep
Had grown for him to vision; and he kept
That sacred vision and the maid thereof
Companions chosen of the peaceful way.
All omens, portents of the natural world
And all the gracious lesser outward signs
Gave up their meanings in the sense of hopes
Which overflow'd him from the world within,
While the two worlds, reacting each on each,
Found both enlarge their borders. So there came
A certain hallow'd noon, when leafy ways
Of woodland labyrinths melted in the light,
And the light sifted through a thousand sprigs
And branches, moving subtly overhead.

Round and about was like a Pentecost,
With little tongues of fire in open spots
Moving and murmuring on the edge of speech.

There—unaccountable, unsought, unknown—
At the fence-side, over against a stile
Which gave on level meads, the meads on brook
Below, the brook upon a hamlet—drawn
About its little ancient church—it fell
That QUÆSTOR DEI and the Master met.

What profit—were it possible—to say
How rose the flimsy veils which first divide
Two strangers, predetermined each on each
To interact? The upward-pointing spire
Seen in the distance, or the slipping burn
Between its bridges, yea, the ravish'd scream
Of lark—song-bursting—hidden in the high
Glory of light—these three or one of these
Could break the bar, could lift so light a yoke
Of silence. Howsoever, in a space
More brief than that which intervened unmark'd
Between the hour and quarter of the old
Church clock, all bonds were melted, and the heart
Of QUÆSTOR DEI to the Master's heart
Was open'd. Here again no word of sleep,
With its strange pageants; and the poet kept—

THE WAY OF THE WATERSIDE

As one whose inmost issues not in words
Even at deep communion, soul to soul—
His tale of agony and endless death
Buried in wells of silence. Might perchance
Recital bring that phantom back to life?
Or was it dead so utterly that words
Could scarce evoke the images? I know
They spoke of symbols and their work in sleep,
Meanings behind them, parables of dream,
Of dreams which lead to vision, but apart
From any vestige of the self therein
On either side of its experience.

For certain days the leading, so begun,
Continued there and here, as seeming chance
Gave out the ways and means. And whatsoe'er
The Master knew of those two inward lives,
He led the other as He led the one
To one same point, which was the Holy Graal
In manifested aspects and in deeps
Withdrawn of hidden meaning. Do I need
To say that both into the heart of heart
Received his message, ponder'd thereupon
And treasured? That which had been long remote,
Some matter of romance—and heard perchance
At second hand, or scarcely heard at all—
Began to live within them and unfold

As light upon familiar ways of sleep.
In part to her who bore the mystic Pyx
There came its message on the verso page
Of life; more fully he beheld who served
The Cup in sleep; but both beheld and read.
So in the light of late experience,
When Pyx and Cup, the woman and the man,
Were brought together, it seem'd—for their two lives—
The Holy Graal was going up and down
The world, as once it went in Arthur's days.

Was it a finding of the Graal for them,
The second advent of the Wounded King,
Himself made whole and bringing healing back
To a wounded world? On many songs to come
The poet dwelt in mind. In mind and heart—
But more and deeper in the secret heart—
BEATA dwelt on life and thought and love,
Hidden within the Hallows of the Cup,
But most upon that moment of the Mass
When priestly hands divide the Sacred Host
And in the consecrated Wine there slips
And sinks one particle of Living Bread.

As if meanwhile his modest part were done
In this first act, the Faithful Master moved

Aside, and in a while the act fulfill'd
Itself. A silent interlude ensued,
And then this drama of a double life
Reopen'd suddenly on wider scenes.

A STAR was mine, and on its throne—
   In kingly state, to earth unknown—
   I ruled star-nations far and wide,
As one who has been deified.
Thou wast not there: too far behind
The compass of my regal state,
I could not hear Thy voice or find
From mine to Thine an open gate.
In chapel, fane and minster fair
Thine altars blazed with flowers and light;
Thine images were everywhere,
Thy worship sounded day and night:
Thou wast not there, Thou wast not there.
A star on earth or star in heaven,
What boots it if all stars be given,
So clouds Thy face of beauty hide?
What boots a crown, and Thou denied?
My throne is vacant and my star
Is left where other signets are:
If Thou be with me, all is mine,
But all is naught till all is Thine;
If Thou be absent, well-a-day,
Stars will not help me on my way.
Better to wait in weeds for Thee
Than rule, a Lord of earth and sea,
Apart from Thee, apart from Thee.

XI

Food of Heaven

THEY pass'd again into the sleep of dream
   And vision; and again they met therein.
A certain consciousness of time elapsed
Was with them, never realized before,
Elusive now, no break in the events
Suggesting, rather some subsurface law
Which interlink'd them on both sides of life
And mark'd one sequence. The next stage of sleep
Would issue therefore from the waking stage
Of being and henceforward lead in turn
Through some assembly of external things
To follow on. But now it came no more—
Did it come ever—with a sense of doom
Unfolding and of actors used therein
As doll's house manikins. Their human will
Had all at once been married to an end
And purpose which in every process spoke
Of Higher Will, shaping with those who shaped

On their own part. O sacred interchange
By which through all the ages of the world
The partnership of God and man directs
The great redeeming work. So souls are led.
So souls obtaining knowledge of themselves
Look back from their attainments and confess
They could not choose but coincide and lead
Their nature-wills to that most perfect point
When they henceforth are taken. Yet the choice
Was theirs, as driven by themselves in love,
Not God-compell'd, Who yet compels by love;
For working with the whole is love's constraint
And an ineffable freedom, love-insured.

Thus are we loosen'd always in the great
High things of being and are bound alone
In law of trifles. God and His good ends
Are reach'd in liberty; the lesser self
Spins ropes, makes rivets, forges heavy chains
To yoke itself, and perishes therein.
Yet from that body of death may the live self
Rise up to vindicate the race thereof,
The freedom and the royalty in God.

The SEEKER-POET and BEATA moved
Amidst the many mansions of the House,
And there was morning in the world without

Its portals. As upon the moon of soul
The self-source light of spirit on a day
Arises and the soul dissolves therein,
To dwell henceforward in the Sun of Christ,
So pass'd for them that quiet moon of dream
Which through the windows of the House had look'd
When soul for soul had lifted veils and thrown
The gates wide open. Morning gold and red
Emblazon'd all the East; and the Sun rose.
It seem'd to both as if that blessed light
Had never shone before on their dream-world.
Dark under stars at times, at others glow'd
The portent of a red unradiant moon,
Low-stooping towards the West, while in the day
Dank vapours blotted out the vault above,
Or at the most the dim light through the clouds
Gloom'd, and perchance—flung through a jagged patch—
Might slantwise fall some transitory gleam.

Now it was light ineffable and now
Glory of living freshness, glory of pearl,
Of rose and amethyst, a second birth
Of Nature. Now the Many Mansion'd House
Received the light without and gave it back
From plinth and pilaster and arch and wall,
While evermore its depths, from space to space,
Open'd, with domes, with chapels and with naves—

An endless Temple. But the Holy Place,
At the imputed East far and away,
Behind a rood-screen and the shining woof
Of a golden curtain, from the vaulted height
To base extended, heal'd its mysteries.

There pour'd forth only an enkindling sense
Of presences; and within, behind, above
That first suggestion, something undeclared,
August and dreadful loom'd. Thereat the heart
Still'd beatings and the offices of thought
Broke on the threshold. Was it of the One
Spirit, withdrawn upon Itself, which gives
Their life to hierarchies whose cohorts fill
The courts, the palaces, the jewell'd streets
Of Zion? Were they facing unawares
A porch of still eternity, or well
Of infinite being, God-head self-immersed,
Which in the spirit-body of the House
Gave notions of immeasurable range?
For those who moved in the soul-part of them
Through aisle or nave, back from the Golden Veil
Self-press'd, were conscious not of awe alone,
Or that which lies too deep for ghostly dread—
But distance past all travel.
                          So it was
With QUÆSTOR DEI and BEATA, brought

FOOD OF HEAVEN

Through many precincts into mighty aisle,
From aisle to nave. The Presence put them back,
Till as from star to star the distance show'd
Between them and the curtain's blazon'd screen
Of glittering cloud. What awful Mercy-seat
Was fix'd behind and through that gorgeous veil
Pour'd rays from GLORIA INHABITANS?
And would that veil at some determined point
Of their advancement open to admit
Their introgression from the Holy Place
Into the utter Adytum, Holiest
Among the Holies?
                    Where a window sprang
From base to height, the risen Sun, above
Pale vapours, and with never lightest cloud
Throughout the welkin, pour'd upon them—there
Kneeling—regenerate glory of its own
And clothed and crown'd them. For a moment, thus
Transform'd, it fell upon the Pyx and Cup,
And there and then, beyond the Golden Veil,
The glory that was ineffable within
Sent down a shaft ineffable and caught
These vessels in the network of the light,
Whereat within the metal began to move
A life which never in the dream before
Had stirr'd and trembled. So the priest-sublimed
In sanctity—on Bread and Wine invokes

G

The life of Christ, the body and the blood,
And life is there.
               The Bearers bow'd their heads
And all was heaven within them for a space,
By thought indrawn. The Bearers rose and stood,
Midwise in nave, while unseen thuribles
Swung round about them, filling the still air
With other incense than ascends on earth,
And in the centre of those hallow'd fumes
Yet sweeter fragrance—not of incense burnt
In heaven or earth—past psychic senses stole,
Till it was with them, for a moment's space,
As when the spirit is alone with God,
In God's great rapture. Incense, solar light,
The golden glory of the Veil, the House
Of Many Mansions in that space dissolved,
And there was neither earth nor very heaven,
But only God; while ravish'd, out of self,
In the love-state of being, they beheld
And were and realized in Him alone—
As love that is, and is alone and one.
So was it, till the glory was withdrawn
Behind the Veil; but this remain'd to shine
With its own splendour, and the blessed sun,
In the salvation of its natural light.
An inward impulse brought the Bearers back
To conscious presence in the Holy House,

Their rapture done: an inner impulse turn'd
Their faces westward. Where the distance—vast
But not beyond our measures—shadow'd forth
A western wall, the Portal of the House
And all its miracle of stone and wood,
Of carvings and of images, they saw
Locming—uncertain, wonderful. With Cup
And Pyx upraised, that impulse prompted still
The Bearers. Passing through the medial space,
The Portal's majesty of breadth and height,
Line upon line of symbol and of saint—
Known and unknown—high messages in words
Heart-flaming, doctrine of all hidden life,
Maxims and mastery of sentences,
Held eyes and mind, their very heart of heart
In homage. So it was a worshipful
Space as of well-deep stillness, whereupon
There supervened a state of hush'd, alert
Expectancy—not silence, for they felt
All chords vibrate within them. New event
Stirr'd on the threshold, and its rumours woke
An answer from their inmost. Not a word
Was utter'd or was needed, for the flash
Of understanding—as through lambent eyes—
From each to each spoke eloquently. Pyx
And Cup yet farther in the shade and light
Were lifted, while the mode and mien of each,

High in the act exalted, swept from grade
To grade of recollection, reverence,
Devotion: this to adoration grew,
Then love—beginning at the human best,
But afterwards transumed, it shone divine.
God's love was in their faces and God's work
Inspired them.
              Now they paused, nor scarcely knew
Of waiting, till the gracious thing to come,
As crossing threshold, on the actual
Emerged. Nor slowly, nor with strident haste
Slipp'd back the Portal's mighty double leaves;
And moving forward—still as those enwrapp'd—
Erect between the pillars of the House
The Bearers stood, like vested priests prepared
For ministry. About the courts and steps
Of that immeasurable edifice,
A multitude of women and of men
Crowded and sway'd: and still the old, old want
Was scored upon their faces. But whereas
That which all recently befell within
Had alter'd aspects in the ways without,
Something had enter'd in those wither'd hearts
And expectation now exceeded want.
Sun-clarity and sheen, with every mark
Of life abounding and world's weal therein,

FOOD OF HEAVEN

Warm'd also these, enlighten'd and bestirr'd
Unwonted pulses, as of ends declared,
Great new beginnings.
                So when those vast doors
Reveal'd the overwhelming nave within,
Whilst the gold curtain's glory glow'd and gleam'd
Where eye could scarcely follow in the far,
An universal sobbing of tremulous hope
And prayer of pent distress went up and down
The concourse. Hush'd into an undertone,
There stirr'd some currents of dead hopes re-born,
Of wonder and desire engirt with awe,
And loosed bonds slipp'd. For which of all had seen
That Temple in old dim-light of the world?
If any, which of them in gloom of night
Or day, had come upon its Portal cast
Open before them, and had look'd therein?

Those Bearers truly through the sad grey land
Had moved and minister'd; but now they stood
Thus, in the nimbus of an aureate light
Transfigured, and the vessels in their hands
Not only gave back glory shining round
But were made quick with splendour of their own—
Subtle, innate and spiritual. Thus
It came about that, prompted suddenly—
As one together—upon bended knees

That congregation fell; and the great work
For QUÆSTOR DEI and BEATA there
And then began. In rapture and in trance
Of ministry, communicating and themselves
Receiving, over and above all signs
Of sacraments, on the morning of that day—
Out of all days taken and set apart—
They fed five thousand in the wilderness
Of morning glory, as with Living Bread
And Wine of Being.   The partakers there
Had very sustenance, to heart's content:
So was there want no longer in that world,
And a deep sense of God within the soul
Was felt abiding. They arose in light
Of innermost refreshment. The old scales
Fell from their eyes, so that for these—as those
Who minister'd—that wilderness whereon
Such Day-Star broke was seen as Paradise;
And a TE DEUM never sung on earth
Peal'd forth triumphant on the lips of all—
The gratitude, the knowledge and the joy
Of such as find that God in very truth
Dwells with His people.   At the end hereof
The House of Many Mansions—in its depth
Of light and grace—received the Bearers back.

The Portals, with a blessing for the world,
Closed on them in a worshipful melody
Of motion; and the conclave thereupon
Was scatter'd on its proper paths and ways.
Each man and woman, to their call in life
Returning, realized the call of God
Therein, so therefore went about His will
And work in peace of the concurring heart.
Peace in the cottage, peace in hall and keep,
The grace of union and the bliss thereof:
O Rose and Lily of that new morning tide,
Feast of the Substance and the Life Divine.
When each partaker had that joy which most
He long'd for served from a most plenteous dish,
Truly the Holy Graal about the world
Was moving, and the end of perilous times,
Of hard adventure, of the want of man,
Had dawn'd, for man was satisfied in God.

So QUÆSTOR DEI and BEATA fed
Their famish'd multitude in a wilderness.

A VISION in the night
    Of a place that is far away,
  On a certain sacred height
Which few can gain: in a secret fane
      At the gospel-side
  Of an altar strangely bless'd
    An open Mass-Book lay.
Till I knew them over and over, again, again
  I have read the words therein;
And now in this aureate Easter morning tide—
Praise God—I have brought them back from the farther side.
    They are words of peace and light;
All other words above, they are words of love:
    They are sacred words of rest.
        Who knows my art? Who knows?
          An altar of repose
  I have made in the heart within.
O Sacred Host, O Wine and Bread,
Those secret things in the heart are said,
And where no foot of man has trod
I have learn'd how to look for God.

XII

A Man and Maid

NOT in the secret paths, or sacred house,
    Built up by hands of men, or any place
Far from the busy turmoil and its haunts;
But just within the free-born country-side,
Rich in a light of summer afternoon,
Among the trees and where a simple stream
Slipp'd through its edges of green herb and grass,
The Blessed Master brought the Man and Maid
Together, and between them took his seat.
No regnant epoch in the life of two
Began more simply. Any story told
Of human lovers, meeting once and then
Inbound for ever, might have found its place
In such a setting. Was his art perchance
For this the greater? If indeed he knew
The secret working of the heart in each
And all the deep misgiving gather'd round
This first encounter of the twain in flesh,

No words betray'd the knowledge, and no words
Did homage to conventions of the world
When they were set together face to face.
How did he shape the normal chance of things
To make them meet? The woman by his side
Was seated haply, or on clover turf
Knelt, as she often did, with her clasp'd hands
Across his knees. Thereafter came the man,
Parting the leafy vintage from behind,
Or down some path's declivity—betwixt
The beech and birch. Some accidents of great
Events stand round them unobserved, and love—
Amidst the epochs in the life of love—
Retains not all the images of that
And this about it. Whether therefore these
Keepers of sacred love within the soul—
And some abysses of experience
Beyond the compass of the name of love
In this our region of similitude—
Did in their hearts preserve the lesser things
Of that deep searching moment, who shall tell?
Not I at least, nor what was firstly said
By him who sat between them. This I know:
On their own part the silence held them each,
But granted such a meeting of true eyes
As spoke more potently than words of earth
On recognition, knowledge held within

And mysteries of being otherwhere
Which each had shared in each.
                          As these flared up
They made a sudden glory of mien and face,
While all suspicions of the faithless past
Fell from their present blessing and no wrack
Of recollection left. It came about,
In high simplicity which seals both worlds,
That—as perchance across the Master's knees—
The hands of each stretch'd over and were clasp'd,
And with a worshipful purity of mouth
They kiss'd each other under the blue sky,
In Nature's happy sunlight. Then it seem'd
That fountain-melodies of hidden birds
Were sprinkling all the spaces, though in truth
They heard them not till coming back to life
Of open senses. So on either side
Of that Wise Master who had shaped their ends
They kept, in silence still, and heard His voice
As if within the singing of the birds,
Like tongues of grace which give to Nature's tones
Another life and meaning.
                          Surely both
Had learn'd already in divided ways,
On his wise part, that which had seem'd to each
Raised up from wells of wisdom lying deep
Within his holy undiscover'd world

Of being. As great poets speak in song
And unmistakable authority
Of inspiration so compels mankind,
It cannot choose but hear, and having heard
Does not alone with clamour of the heart
Make answer, but the very heart of some
Seems speaking in the music and the words,
Until the poet's messages become
A part of life and ready on the lips
Are pass'd for evermore from mouth to mouth:
So QUÆSTOR DEI and BEATA heard
Of old, with every pulse arrested, then
With pulses quicken'd, then with far prolong'd
Heart beatings, then with stillness of the heart,
And finally with fully waken'd soul,
Responding both in silence and in speech,
And from the midmost and the very ends
Of their two natures filling with the light
Of understanding, as all heaven and earth
Are fill'd with light at noon.
                                      This for the past,
This for its sever'd ways, for dowers therein.
But in the present linking of their lives
It was as though some intervening bar,
Unnoticed, had been raised. They knew not how,
They knew not what: this only standing forth—
That something potent here unloosed and freed

The Master's tongue, Who spoke as never yet
He spoke to either in divided days—
From such deep places of experience.

He might have lifted up anointed hands
At that great Altar's eastern end, when they
Stood looking towards each other in the House
Of Many Mansions; might have moved between
The Bearers passing down the Temple's nave
To feed the hungry in the wilderness.
What other House—or so it seem'd to them—
But that which vision had reveal'd and led
Their souls within, was limn'd by burning words,
He speaking of the hidden head and font
Of spiritual mysteries, a House
Not made with hands, a Temple whence the grace
And knowledge flow to sanctify the world
In and by Christ, the Spirit and the Man,
The Immanent Divinity shown forth
In human nature? Known by many names,
Far up and down the ages and the world,
Its echoes and reflections of the life
Divinely hidden in the heart of God
Had spread. House of the Spirit, Hidden Church,
The School of Heaven and Brotherhood elect:
Therein abides the Christ Who once on earth
Was Chief and Crown of all the Messengers.

The earthly Master, hail'd in heart as such
By both his hearers, though no claim of his
Assumed the title, though he pass'd indeed
On many missions bearing a plain name—
That witness testified concerning Him
Who still is Master here on earth, in heaven
And in the underworld, for those who call
On His great Name, and for all chosen souls
Under the ægis of the Christian world.
House, Palace, Temple, howsoever styled,
The Sanctuary of His Presence, when He walks—
Seen or unseen, but ever seen in heart—
Amidst the Blessed Company and School
Is that most sacred source of valid grace
Which flows through all the Sacraments of Grace
And Nature.
            Thus with power the Master spoke
As one proficient in the secret things
Of high communication and the modes
By which the world derives not only life
But sustenance. To two of all that world
The timeless certitude behind such words
Gave what the message, of this power deprived,
Could not itself impart, the seal of one
Who from the centre of experience
Came forth to witness, who had dwelt within
That hidden Temple, realized and shared

The presence of that Immanence Divine
Which is the core of this created world.

After a space wherein the stillness seem'd
Like Nature sleeping in the arms of God,
Or like the calm activity of God
Within the sacramental veil of things
Made manifest—so that his hearers touch'd,
For that brief moment in their waking state
The vibrant centre of essential life—
Again the Blessed Master spoke and said:

"Beyond that Temple there is unity,
And Thou and I, changed over from this mode
Of being which abides in self of self,
Are henceforth bosom'd in the self of God,
Know Him, and are deliver'd from the bond
Of our own knowing. He is All in all,
And we in Him, no more from all apart,
Are integrated with the whole in all.
The world's great joy is with us and within,
While our self-joy is in the mighty world.
Here is the true theopathy of rest
And here the true activity, at once
'Divine event' and that which works thereto,
And—being raised—uplifts the lesser things,

With all that in creation moves to reach
Beatitude, perfection, mastery.
So come we at the end into our own
And this receives us."
                        On his hearers fell
Another stillness, as of inward soul.
The Master's voice had died, or if He spoke
They knew not. The enlightening word became
The silence, but the light therein shone out,
Dissolving and transfiguring. All stir
Of Nature fell away in one last chord,
And this was hush'd. Ineffably those twain
Were pour'd together; each became in each
One ens transcendant. They were poised therein
Almost across the threshold of a state
Which was but prefaced in the Holy House.
Great issue of an instant from the known
Of being's aspects, in such flash of time
That pass'd which was not of itself contain'd
In measures of duration.
                        Then the tones
Of Nature's voices enter'd once again
By normal avenues of sense. The twain—
A little dazed—for one more moment saw
Creation with the focus of their eyes
Striving to readjust. Thereafter came
The Master's voice, while his right hand was lock'd

A MAN AND MAID

Within the two hands of the Man and Maid.
Once more in soul or spirit he might have stood
Between them, they bearing the Pyx and Cup
In their dream-place of holy mystery.
Then the diaphanous brightness of the world
About them—and the beauty everywhere
Purified and uplifted—gave them back,
Through all their channels, a still vaster sense
Of Temple and of Sanctuary. Behind
Their veils—which any moment, in between
The Master's words, might lift or melt away—
The sacred cosmos quiver'd to disclose
The sacred place of true experience,
The Holy of the Presence—not indeed
To eyes of flesh, nor even eyes of soul,
But heart within the soul and heart of hearts.
The Master speaking of the Master Christ
Said that He came carrying Bread and Wine.
These were His visible symbols; these He raised
From signs of Nature into signs of Grace,
To manifest analogies betwixt
The food of body and the food of souls,
The nutrimental matter of the world
And that God-substance lying hid therein,
Its life and essence. So these two dissolve
One into other; so the Daily Bread
Becomes as Bread of Angels; so the Wine

Which cheers and fortifies the natural man
May also be the Wine of Other Life
Unto the man within. The pregnant scheme
Of sign and symbol, for all those who dwell
In the two worlds without dividing them
But equally partaking, is maintain'd
In marriage union with that noumenal
Which signs show forth. The Eucharist is thus
A bond between the worlds, for this bequeathed,
A link of union in the height and deep.
The Spirit of the Christ remains therein
On every altar and in every soul
Which can receive the Spirit. So is God
Made man in Christ, and so the Word takes flesh
Through all the ages. There is Bethlehem
In every kingdom, country, shire and town.
The world itself is Nazareth. Each man
And woman in the body-part of them
Is Bethlehem's stable. But the soul therein
Is seldom Mary, bearing Christ within.
Hence is the Hidden Church from age to age
In travail, working towards that perfect day
When Christ shall have been born of every soul,
Or when the soul shall know the Christ within,
And the most blessed offices of Bread
And Wine shall reach fulfilment. Then the soul—
God-tinctured, God-transmuted, God-possess'd—

Shall need these signs no more. Till that great day
The Hidden Church has sent out messengers
With rumours of a noumenal Eucharist,
Doctors and saints and mystics more than all.
But once through legend and through high romance
The Secret Church sent out the Holy Graal.

After these words that kind of silence fell
Which indicates the end of things attain'd,
Or their suspension for some given time.
The hearers look'd into their Master's face
And saw how joy was also peace therein.
He link'd their hands together, rose and then
Standing behind them rather than between,
While they two drew together, his own hands
Extended, blessing silently, and left
By the ascending path between the trees:
The trees received the Master out of sight.

IN the morning of life,
 But the morning was sombre and sad:
  There was mist upon valley and street
   And sadly, with wearyful feet—
How pale in the morning of life—
  Came love, full of tears, to the lad.
   I did not know it, and woe is me,
    Thus early and only I look'd for Thee.

In the noonday of life
  There came with a crown to the man,
   Strong, stedfast and starry of birth,
   A love for the life of earth—
So fair in the noonday of life—
  To dwell on the earth for a span.
   Great gifts are gracious, such gifts were given:
   But, Earthly Love, what of Love in Heaven?

In the evening of life,
  In an ashen glow, on a path alone,
   It was Thou, Whom I look'd for from first to last:
   I found Thee, I have Thee, I hold Thee fast—
Soul-Lord in the evening of life—
  Thine be my leading through ways unknown:
   They are known in Thee; they are paths above;
   In the arms which enfold me, all paths are love.

XIII

Of Spiritual Marriage

THOSE whom a strange election had in sleep
    Granted a grade of union never reach'd
In earthly nuptials—or if reach'd indeed
By some few souls, no record rests on earth—
Thus left together, having hand in hand,
Look'd once again into each other's eyes;
As soul in soul had look'd when purposed dream
Had grown to vision, after gates unbarr'd
And veils uplifted. Now the eyes of both
Show'd deeps within and light upon the deeps;
But eyes of flesh are not true doors of soul,
While fleshly veils do not in waking states
Strip off their vestures. So perchance for this
They did not kiss in solitude, who kiss'd
At their first greeting. When the witness sat,
A golden link of spirit them between,
His presence meted freedom in the heart.

No yoke constrain'd them now; but something pass'd,
And in the precincts left its place unfill'd,
With him. Awhile the sunlight and green leaves
Were things of Nature to herself return'd,
Not seen in trance of spiritual joy.
Mayhap the greeting kisses to their own
Drew added sanctity of grace and light
From springs within the Master, while apart
From him that high observance—for a space—
Seem'd best held over. Whether best or not
I rule in no wise, since by many ways
Soul reaches soul. However, so they sat,
True lovers, unto whom external signs
Of love incarnate and the house of flesh
In scant wise profited. A little while,
And they were speaking of their state in dream,
Together drawing on the outward side
From more to more.
                          Withal a certain sense
Of want unsatisfied, of cloud in thought,
Or such disparity, had breathed betwixt
And importuned the consciousness of both.
How light a sense, how very rare a veil,
Was best, I think, exhibited when each
Found ready terms in freedom thereupon
And earn'd, moreover, in the speech exchanged
An interlinking like the state of soul

In sleep, however far the distance stretch'd
To make a phantom of comparison.

She gave him both her hands. He took them both
In sudden silence momently. To him
And her it was at once as if a queen
Had offer'd hands and in the act became
Earth-queen no longer but of sacred realms
Explored in part, while other worlds beyond
Stretch'd through the undiscover'd. Unto her
And him it was as though a priest and king
Came out of Salem, carrying Bread and Wine,
The healing of the nations in his hands.
And she acclaim'd him ever in her heart
Priest of the Most High God. They knelt anon,
Facing each other, while the falling sun
Cast slantwise beams upon them and betwixt,
And made another glory in the world,
Transmuting gold to amber, building up
Nimbus on nimbus, crown and aureole,
Till all the simple blossoms of the wild—
Daisy and buttercup and celandine—
Shone round them, gleaming, glowing on the sward,
Then changing suddenly to things most rich,
Most rare.
        So was it, and again to both
Transfigured Nature, full of radiant dyes,

Discover'd pageants by the world at large
Unseen, beyond the violet and the red,
Glamour ineffable of gorgeous hues,
Of tints betwixt the purple and the blue,
Orange and yellow, like a soul within
Great Nature, pouring from behind all bands
And lines and crannies. Out of grassy nest
A bird sprang up and in the middle heaven
Scream'd high Graal overture of melody,
And hidden runnels by the path and hedge
Began to speak in silver undertones
Intelligibly. No longer in the world
Did hearts which "need a language" seek in vain.
All spoke, and in the tongue native to each—
From summer breeze between the leaves, from loud
And resonant organ-tones over the hills,
To whatsoever moved and what was still
Far over earth. Places of silence spoke,
And that which spoke gave silence to the heart,
While very stillness profited in speech
To ears of soul.
    So was it and would be:
But at that moment when they look'd and saw,
About the mauves and ochres of the hills
Which made their jewell'd ring on that world's verge,
The changing splinter'd light of many rays

Flung there and here, a thousand little tongues
Of lambent fire and light flickered and fled,
Or dwelt and hover'd up and down the slopes,
And there was flowing as of streams of light,
While round and through the pillars of the piled
Upland on upland in the middle West,
An opening for the departing sun
Reveal'd a cosmic heart of ardent fire
Beneath abysses of green. Hereat the wind
Veer'd suddenly, pour'd forth its warm life-breath,
Till there was Pentecost for those two hearts,
Once and henceforth for ever in the world.
In that great moment's glory, suddenly struck
Out of the open globe—as fire from flints—
They might have raised their voices, kneeling still,
Amidst the mystic pentecostal tongues.
But there were harps sounding within the spheres
Of each, to hold them silent, and they heard
That tongue of tongues which has no voice on earth,
An utterance of the cosmic word within—
Infinite love, infinite melody,
The very root of all the life in life
Of earths and worlds.
     So the misfaith and doubt
Utterly perish'd. Those who met in soul,

And not till later in the body of each,
Knew one another, nor beheld therein
That real things were very far away;
But rather for the work of dream in sleep
And work of waking vision there was reach'd
A certain centre, a most holy ground
To build on. It foreshadow'd—as on verge
Of living knowledge—that those dual states,
Reacting on each other, should produce
An end of being, welded, unified,
Which never surely in divided life
Of outward sense or inward deeps might reach
Such measure of fruition. Therefore flesh,
Seen in this light of spiritual things,
Profited something. Not as through a glass
And darkly, in the common life of earth,
They look'd at one another, for the world
And mundane light, transfigured from within
Their own transmuted natures, enter'd now
Another grade of dignity and wore
New robes of glory. When the parting came,
For that or this allotted space of time,
They would not leave unsatisfied but fill'd,
And with no hunger in the world henceforth
Awaiting them.
     The hour of sunset came
And in the evening purples and the puce,

Amidst the lifted thuribles which smoked
In answer to the falling dews and gave
A temple-scent like unto breath of life,
They stood together and were folded up
In one another's arms. It was again
Two souls which met and kiss'd and interlock'd,
While all the motions and desires of flesh
Went up to God, like incense born of dews
From weeds and flowers about them. Heaven's blue dome,
Out of its phosphor, brought forth liquid stars—
Like Sons of God in contemplation still
And vibrant, full of witness and of joy.
All weary burdens of the world of sin,
Letting and hindrance, fell from off their hearts.
In love's great worship and high reverence
The blessed goodness of the Lord of Good
Was with them in the Land of Living Things.

So they were married in their hearts of flesh,
To ratify a union in the soul
By rite most perfect, catholic and pure,
Beyond all need of ministry from man,
All consummations which the outward rites
Do consecrate for earthly needs and ends,
Nor yet reducing offices of these
And holy sacraments of outward Church,

Or laws of state, but entering withal
A world of higher measures, hidden life
Of union, intercourse of nuptial souls,
As fully seal'd in the external ways
By marriage intercourse of mouth and mouth,
Or arms in arms, as by the five pure points
Of fellowship in nuptial modes of earth,
And with the centre.
                  When the night had come
They parted on their proper earthly ways
And made no covenants of meeting, there
Or here, well knowing that the world of dream
Should give them back the Altar and the House,
The Bearers' Office and the Rite therein,
While in the world of those who think they wake—
But are encompass'd by another sleep
Until they waken both in dream and life—
Unmeasured vistas, stretch'd through place and time,
Held opportunities at every point
For meetings and renewals. Which of these
Should most befit the purpose of their days
That blessed purpose would itself declare;
And in the perfect certitude hereof,
Each looking only in the eyes of each
And each commending each to God's true care,
They left—and look'd not back—in holy joy.
The Master, leading over earthly ways,

Stood in the middle night, and the great dome
Of starry heaven watch'd with him, when the world
Was sleeping. As it might be, from a peak
He watch'd the city and its ways of men—
I know not: or the city was asleep
And with the stars he watch'd, as it might be,
On tower or lonely parapet or bridge—
I know not. Wheresoever, unto stars—
With eyes uplifted and extended arms—
He reach'd out, inly worshipping, in trance
Of thought imploring. Then beyond the stars,
Out of all signs, transported in pure mind,
His soul soar'd through the Immanence Divine
To God transcendent, and enfolded there
His wordless prayer was fix'd upon the end
Towards which his son and daughter of desire
Were taken—in some part surely by him
But for the rest by the invisible
Keepers of mysteries. Be they drawn and brought
Thereby within the shelter of its arms,
As he was drawn unsearchably and found
A place within the palace and the shrine.

At that ineffable centre which fulfils
In oneness the within and the without
Be God discern'd not only of their hearts

And known of soul, but He abide in them
And they in Him, a perfect being-state
At once of God in all and all in God.

Beyond the prayer of rapture and the prayer
Of silence drawn into a deeper mode,
The Master's soul within the centre held,
And with the Eternal Spirit Which is Christ
Made one therein, far past all images
And individual forms of him and her,
Knew QUÆSTOR DEI and BEATA fix'd
Henceforth and perfectly contain'd therein,
While in the Immanent and Transcendent God—
By hypostatic union and the bond
Of love between Them, Which is Spirit of all—
They all, and Christ together, render'd up
The Kingdom of separate things—from time's divorce
And substitution finally redeem'd—
Into the Father's hands. And this is that
Wherein God's end of being and of things
Describes the perfect circle and returns
To that beginning where the circle falls
Within the centre.
                      Having seen and known
The eternal hope for those he led in truth,
That centre gave the Master back to life,
While in the East the red and saffron dyes

Brought in another morning, breaking forth
Upon a sleeping world.
                        The Master hail'd
With reverential eyes and worshipful
Heart, the new glories of God's day proclaim'd,
And took and did God's business in the day.

GLORY of cosmic pageants, glory and grace of all:
   Have I not dwelt among them? How should they weary or pall?
The great processions go on, in their rhythm of stately joy:
I walk among them and with them, or stand for a space aside,
In a contemplation deep—perchance where the ways divide.
In truth I am looking for Thee; and where the banners deploy—
Is it there that Thou art? Or else in the gulf as of fire,
Where the orange and purples open out the heart of their great desire?
Or the starry dark of a sacred night eastward suddenly lightens?
Who knows? I listen, I hear: the music crashes and heightens.
There are seasons also of stillness, the pause of a peace that falls,
And the only voice in the silence is that of the heart which calls.
A sleep comes over the pageant; the mystery-plays suspend:
It is Thou perchance in the stillness: is it Thou, at the journey's end?
Ah, no! Save only in rumours, in portents behind a veil,
I do not reach Thee in pageants, and their pomp at last, like a tale
That is told, has given its message. Behold, I have lived in their light:
Beyond these symbols, my End, my Need, call me to worlds of sight.

XIV

Priest and Priestess

BEFORE the rood-screen and the veil thereof
   The Pyx and Chalice of the Bearers stood,
   Clear-shining in the light which pierced the Veil,
For now there rose upon its hither side
A double cube of well-white marble, graved
In gold with words and names and hidden signs,
A mystic Altar by the Holy Place;
And prompted by the monitor within
They set their vessels down.
                        As when they met
On life's awakening side for that first time,
Remembering a vigil in the past,
Wherein the other side of life in sleep
Forth-issued out of sleep—and what is named
Deep dream—into a being-state of soul,
Whereof all waking they had known should count
Mere shadow of reality, so now—
In vision and its open images—

Their souls recall'd that meeting in the world
Of outward icons, what it proved for them
Beyond the doubting foresight of the heart;
How mortal flesh began to feel and see
The wonder and the glory of the world;
And how the mind incorporate therein
Itself had entered on a being-state,
Of which all measures through the past made known
Were also shadows of reality.
They, standing therefore upon either horn
Of that white Altar, and themselves in light,
From living light which dwelt beyond the veil,
Began to realize that both the states
Were at their root of purpose one within.
Yet some swift-flying question pass'd through both:
Whether the waking state of body and soul,
With union reached therein, while soul and soul
Preserved but rarefied the outward part,
Had not a wholeness which the vision state
Wanted, and whether individual will—
Which shaped its ends on earth—were not for them
A truer state than this most ghostly scene.
Herein they moved as something not themselves
Directed, whether from them apart or not,
And—in the high Rite integrated—shared
No forming purpose midst activities

Thereof. Only when motived pageant ceased
Their part with one another intervened.
Then it was will, activity, a state
Of seeing in worlds on worlds, opening out
And into one another, while the things
Beheld—ineffably, essentially—
Were one with that which saw; and in a mode
Beyond all time the Everlasting Love
Was its own object.
                But this moment pass'd,
While that which follow'd ravish'd from their souls
All notion of the personal part in them,
All speculation of the mind, all sense
Of place, of motive, operation there.
They knew thenceforward that the Master-Lord
Was in the many-mansion'd House, a still,
Abiding Presence; and with one intent—
To find Him, see Him, worship Him therein—
They went on quest, scarce knowing what they did,

As inly spurr'd, unconscious that they moved—
In being's keen awareness, stripp'd of self.
The Temple grew before them; but its halls,
Chapels and chambers, vast scriptoria,
Its stairways—often as to height of stars
Ascending—and its secret doors which gave,
At unsuspected angles, upon roofs

Like platforms stretching through uplifted planes—
To them concentred, burning for the end—
Were not the mighty measures of a House,
Whether by hands erected or drawn out
In spiritual spaces, but the states
And pregnant epochs of the master-quest—
How long pursued who knows, Master and Lord?

They met with spokesmen of the Mysteries
Who saw the Master daily in the House,
And said: Lo, here or there, turning to East
And West, proclaiming gospels in His Name
And bearing certain warrants in their hands,
A proof of embassy; while other some
On ancient books depending saw therein
His first and final message, whence they preach'd
Obedience, witnessing of penalties
And great rewards. For such the Master's House
Was not alone a Temple built with hands
But raised by them or their progenitors.
A few upon some spiritual side
Of lower grooves depended. These affirm'd
The earth His Temple, and that which seem'd a House
All profitless till spiritually known,
When chancel, altar and the Holy Place,
With any Rites enacted these within,

Would pass like shows and leave the soul with God—
Not seen or realized, but joined in thought
By moral bonds together. There and here—
Rarest of all—a few with faces seal'd
By perfect stillness, and with light thereon
Forth shining, like the light behind the Veil,
From inward source, the arms upon their breasts
Folded, went up and down, speaking no word,
Or in the Veil's glow waited, worshipping.
These also, often on their knees received
From Pyx and Chalice, at the Bearer's hands,
The Bread and Wine, in recollection merged;
And then the lambent flickering of light
About the vessels got another mode
Of lustre—a fix'd, penetrating glow—
As if all sunbeams had been focuss'd there.

Two vessels looking like two Graals of grace,
Two Bearers, a procession of the Graal
Concentred, priest and priestess of a Rite
According to Melchizedek—Priest and King—
Kept secret age on age, were here and now
Made in the holy hiddenness manifest
To two or three, in the Great Name and Word
Gather'd together. But a thousand pass'd
For whom the Veil was just a curtain's height;

The man and maid were priests in ritual-guise
Performing sacramental ministries;
And these meant little. Of such questers, some
Beyond the ceremonial and its form
Had pass'd in thought; some held them worshipful
But done in memory; and when the Graals
Swept down the chancel, in the Bearer's hands
Uplifted, shedding the strange light of them,
Some saw the works of miracle and cried
With open mouths. These follow'd from behind,
Looking beyond the portals, where the crowd
Were fed with Wine and Bread, or mix'd themselves
With these, thereafter—up and down the land—
Preaching the Kingdom and the coming Christ,
But understanding little in the heart,
And hence from one distraction over soon
To other flowing, like a shallow stream,
At every point diverted.
                        Now it came
To pass, after a day of many days
Perchance, that QUÆSTOR DEI and the Maid,
BEATA MEA, on the Guide within
Depending, ceased their quest about the House
To find the Blessed Master and High Lord,
But waited—watching over Pyx and Cup—
Because when toiling feet of body or soul

Have wearied, vainly seeking up and down,
The air about them as the heart within
May with a holy suddenness give up
The Blessed Master and the end of quest.

I HAVE borne my part in the Temples,
   The solemn state of each;
I have shared in the lyrical dramas
   By action, song and speech.
I have follow'd the holy functions
   Wherever their Rites have call'd,
As one for those ends anointed,
   Exalted and install'd.
I have held both Warrant and Charter,
   And where Grand Masters sat,
Throned high in the eastern quarter,
   I have join'd the debate on that
     Which attests the Mastery.
It is all of it great and good
   To share and hear and see;
And if in the heart—as now—
   I ask whether these are Thine,
   The answer is: Surely Mine.
But when I proceed: Is it Thou?
A stillness falls on the vibrant halls
   And a hush on the Holy place:
   They have echoed from roof to base,
     But only with rumours of Thee.

O House and Temple and Lodge,
   Upon all your craft and art
I crave the grace of a blessing
   And join with thankful heart,
Or ever we take the Closing
   And so from such walls depart.
I have dwelt in your shaded spaces,
Have shared their guerdons and graces
   To the very end and the essence;
True signs of the grand totality
   Are raised up in divers places:
But Give me, O God, the reality,
   One light of all in the Presence.

XV

A Golden Veil of Doctrine

THEY are with their Master in the waking state:
   He sits again betwixt them and—with hands
   Uplifted—teaches in the vesper-time.
A humble country chapel's chancel steps
Are now the place of meeting. Whether he
Was priest therein they did not ask or know.
Far other speculation fill'd their minds,
While on his head the Sanctuary Lamp
Cast faint and peaceful light through ruby glass,
Weaving an aureole about his face
And wool-white hair. As they in life assumed
But in the sleep-state and its dreams laid flesh
Aside, yet were the same—one self in each
Amidst all variations in their mode
Of being and changes of environment—
So Christ, the Master, Whom they sought in soul
Perchance was he, no other, who without
Had come of his own will into their lives.

Shaped he their paths of vision who show'd forth
True ways of practice in the daily round?
When they should meet him in the hidden world
Would he be other than he seem'd and was
Betwixt them, seated in the twilight-tide?
And would the hallows of the Pyx and Cup
Shine at his presence with another light
Than earth's or soul's, a very light of God
Dwelling with man?
                      Now from the Sacred Host
Within the tabernacle's silken veil
There fell upon them that which was not light
But influx—out of holy heaven sent down—
Or rather upon him it seem'd to fall
And from two centres, at his heart and head,
Was ray'd within them. Such a Presence fill'd
The Church of Nature when he sat before—
Green vistas round them. But even more than then
His words transfigured all things: so of old
At Cana, water from the springs of earth
Became a wine which never in the world
Gave forth the vintages of Galilee.
Light from the Graal about them, words of God
Exhibited His Mysteries in speech
Of man, nor ever any human speech
Was simpler. Like a blessed gospel-text

A GOLDEN VEIL OF DOCTRINE

Which holds the high vibrations of the life
From the life-source outpour'd, it held the tones
And chants and breathings of the world within—
High sanctuary of hidden heart of things.
So therefore drew the music wrought in words
Into a single sense of harmony,
Even as the Spirit Divine draws human souls
And makes a oneness of eternal state
Which is the perfect poem of each soul
And its life-ode.
     Of that most sacred House
Which seem'd their House of Vision and perchance
Was of its modes and aspects shown in part—
So mighty texts of old in modern tongues
Are put by moderns—again the Master spoke,
Of its high rumours moving down and up
The realms of thought and history. Betwixt
That side of things wherein the letter rules,
Nor ever of itself uplifts a veil—
Because the veil it is, which cannot pass
Beyond its nature—and that other mode
Lying behind, spirit and inward sense,
The Holy House is poised, as on a space
Which serves for borderland where the two worlds
Converge, itself an interlinking bond.
There type in antitype dissolves and there
The simple letter is itself a sign.

O central point and sacred meeting-place
Of all the sacraments, there falls the Bread,
Broken within the Wine-Cup, and from both
Issues one living Spirit of Life Divine.
Never was place or house more deeply hid
Within the souls of those who dwell therein.
No temple ever was a part of mind
As thou, mind-sphered in pure intelligence!
No secret palace is enshrined like thee
Within the heart, for thou art love thereof,
Lo, in this House of God, soul, mind and heart
Are found in oneness at the root of each—
One vesture of that Spirit which is God,
One eye which looks on God—but turn'd within—
One fire by God enkindled, evermore
Burning in Him, consumed, renew'd by Him,
But He the substance, He the flame and He
The kindling spark.   Hereof the Secret House
And its deep searching. So beneath the fields—
Yellow with harvests under a bright sun—
Lie hid the gold and jewels of the mine,
Crypts and great treasure of the under-world.
See then, till all the images dissolve—
Their order and their laws fulfill'd in God—
Here is the common ground of those who pass
Beyond the veils into the first great sense

Which lies behind. This is the Holy House
In sacramental things externalized
And sum as such of all the sacraments.
The signified is not without the sign
Therein. The inward and the outward make
A marriage, integrated more and more
In one another while the worlds endure,
Till that which now is the without for us
Becomes by sanctity's dissolving work
That which we call within. Then God's great end—
Which stands and knocks without the cosmic gates—
Shall find all gates are open and come in.

The House is theirs who have attain'd in Christ,
By His own blood redeem'd, for blood is life,
Eternal life, and so is understood
In the deep symbols of this mystery.
He leads the sons thereof from state to state
Of that Divine Experience within
Forth shadow'd once in holy, holy veils—
The pageant of the Life in Palestine.
A Birth Divine, a hidden life in God,
And then the witness of an outward call;
The mystic passion, cross and death thereon;
The resurrection and ascent in God:
Herein stands forth the story of the soul,
From that first moment which is second birth

To that last stage ineffable when man
Goes back to God.
     The Many-Mansion'd House
Presents in type the state before the end,
The resurrection-life attain'd in Christ.
So is it Holy Zion in the Heights,
Palace of Peace and the Great Prince of Peace,
The Paradise and Highest Court of Heaven.
Those dwell therein who may have tasted death
In bodies of earth or may in fleshly bonds
Abide and wait upon deliverance;
But mystic death has made them free in Christ.
So is the end assured, and thus they dwell
In unity, knowing their part in Him,
The present which is He, the state to come
And consummation of their life in God.

Within the Sacred House there also dwell
That Company of Spiritual Chiefs
And Hierarchs, through the ages set to watch
And through continued ages guard and guide
The long succession of a royal race
Whose secret once was mask'd as David's line—
A priestly work which, when the days were full,
Brought Joseph forth, the heir in fine of all,
And from another dynasty, to earth
As earth unknown, in Blessed Mary found

For him a virgin mate, with mystic yoke
Of nuptials in the Holy Heart of things,
Not in the heart of flesh. So came in fine
That Incarnation which was Birth Divine,
An union of the Spirit and the Bride
In earthly house of man—or body of God—
Made manifest. So He Who is the Word
In flesh abode among us, and the types
Of this substantial union are in Church,
In wayside Chapel and in mighty Fane
Shown forth—a true analogy of things—
By Bread and Wine. The Secret Church above
Is antitype of all the speaking signs
And sacraments, the treasury of grace
And power which fills them, permeates, overflows
In the recipient's heart.
      Because of grace,
Of sanctity, of thinking in the heart,
Of Eucharistic Life Divine, which some
Reach'd there and here, ascending from the world
Of symbols to the power and glory held
Within, a rumour went about the earth
And bare its witness to the Holy House
In many modes of doctrine and of thought,
In many miracles of Wine and Bread,
After the mode of legend told from one
To other. In most sacred openings

Of sacramental veils, whereat dissolved
The elements, exhibiting behind
Divine communions and the Word therein,
Some part was given of God's grace and truth
To hidden life of soul.
     Hereby began
Great inquests up and down the Christian world.
High reason follow'd them in holy schools
Of doctrine, though the letter overlaid
That witness. There were also secret ways
Of league and fellowship—in open words
Some speaking, other some a hidden tongue
Of symbol. There was more than all that school
Of saintship lifted into sovereign realms
Of a Divine Experience reach'd within,
And this left glorious records, shining still—
Beacons to those who in this narrow path
Can follow and ascend the Mount of God.
Such was in fine the spirit in that past
Of single-hearted centuries, that the quest
Was follow'd also and the tidings came
Through great imagination's shaping modes,
And—out of expectation—fair romance
Became a vehicle and thus put forth
The Holy Graal. I think—the Master said—
Old stories now are preface to a new
Romance of soul, which shall be told henceforth

Of yesterday, to-day and evermore,
With all the Mystery disclosed therein.

So fell the Master's teaching once again
To silence, and his hearers' hearts were fill'd
With that high worship which election brings.
But evermore they wonder'd—each with each,
Or inwardly, in humbleness of heart—
What power and mercy should have singled such
As they, two children of obscurity,
For so high ends. Now in the outward ways
Full often meeting—since the walls of things
Dissolved about them upon every side
And brought the pair together day by day—
They heard the Holy Masses of the Church,
And peace was with them. Many graces stood
Around them, enter'd through their open doors
And vivified. Yet of the secret things
Behind the Eucharist—the while endured
This further space of interlude between
The teaching of the Blessed Master's mouth
And that of vision—no great message came,
Fair intimations to the mind at work
Or held in stillness.
                    Knowing as they did
That in their other, hidden side of life
They served an Altar, like the priest on earth,

But out of earthly things to those of soul
Raised up, and were enring'd on every side
With witness of the Presence; knowing too
How in the spiritual House they bare
The self-same elements of Bread and Wine;
What hidden bond subsisted at the root
Between the sacred work imposed on them
And that of ministers in outward ways
Ordain'd? No ordination save of work
Imposed by service had the active life
Of their strange sleep set as a seal on them.
No consecration had their lips or hands
Perform'd, though since the Many-Mansion'd House
Roll'd back its portals and receiv'd them in,
They knew what sacro-saintly life abode
Within the Bread and Wine they bare and gave
To crowds of worshippers who knelt without
And some who follow'd on the quest within.

Now, both were conscious—in distinctive ways—
Of inward trouble, dwelling on the place
And pageant of their vision life, and all
Its purpose, in comparison with that
Which earthly paths had in these later days
Assumed. How also did the House within
Stand in relation to the visible Church
Of God? And seeing that in deeper states

A GOLDEN VEIL OF DOCTRINE

Within they found the well of images
Reduce its wealth of parabolic modes,
While on the threshold of a time they seem'd
To stand when all the pageants and the forms
Should cease, and knowledge of the noumenal
Be reach'd in being-state—pure, simple, free
And undiversified, the old mental sight,
The tactions and auditions set aside
Once and for all—perchance at end of things
The speaking drama of the world of dream
Would into teaching parable resolve
And so discharge its purpose. Who should say?
But only when the waking world dissolved,
The words which spoke within them still convey'd
That counsel, Patience, and that caution, No:
Not yet.
   Now, whether in the part of flesh
I know not, or in that half-seeming state—
Say, after lips had sever'd, holy hands
Still interlock'd—when the white ivory gates
Began to open, while all thoughts and things
Strangely converged and mix'd, it matters not:
I do not know; but in each other's arms,
After a pure and spiritual mode,
They fell asleep into a world unknown,
And reach'd, apart from any sense of place,
Another state of vision, soul to soul

Reveal'd, and each as an unspotted glass
Wherein they look'd together and beheld
Not deeps of one another, but their own.
By such a perfect interchange of love,
Out of the House of Life and House of Sleep,
They knew the oneness, waking one with dream,
One soul in twain, and at the root conjoin'd
With one Christ-Spirit of the Word and God,
Looking in Him to reach all end of quest.

For QUÆSTOR DEI and BEATA may
The veils lift further. May their sleep indeed
Be fill'd with vision. May they find within
One Spouse of both, and so for evermore
Be and continue one in each and Him:
Not QUÆSTOR DEI and BEATA now—
In that great, timeless, everlasting now—
Not Christ and they, or Christ and one from them
Begotten by the motherhood of love,
But union, unity and oneness, Christ
As they in Him, and He in them, yet God
In all ineffably, and all in God.

THEY taught me many doctrines, and I made
Due acts of faith in loyalty and laid
Their freight upon me, till a Voice arose
And said: All blessing on the man who knows
The matter of the one true faith and thence
Draws sacred doctrine of experience.
Now, since my hope was in one Source and End,
I held that Voice a Comforter and Friend.
So, having put aside all yokes, I sought
In sacred licence of untramell'd thought
On mountain-heights of mind to reach my Goal.
And past all peaks of thought I saw the soul,
And in her hidden world I strove to find
That which exceeds all altitudes of mind.
Ah, but the soul that Presence may confess
Through intimations which their seals impress,
As light on earth impinged from furthest star.
Hence from the soul herself the Goal was far,
Till in her heart of love a certain door
I open'd, with a permit to explore;
And there the Goal my efforts could not win—
O Master-Goal—reach'd out and took me in.

XVI

Christ Mystical

THE waiting inquest in the House of Sleep
And House of God continues—not in vain.
Apart from outward sign or inward word
By still assurance silently infused,
They knew that as the Master seen on earth
Was in His proper time and mode declared,
So too the Temple's Master—not on earth
Or in the Temple's outer court of heaven
Beheld—must in a fitting hour and way,
After the order of the things of soul,
To them be manifest, and then should lead
To whatsoever hiddenness of God
Abides behind the glory and the veil
Of gold. The lesser pageants of the quest
Moved round them in the many-sided House;
Their own great Rite continued day by day,
As days are counted in the world of dream.
Yet in the midst of all, from all apart,

Far and still farther they explored in thought
And in that loving contemplation which
Suspends most highest thought—upon the gulf
Poised, tranced and quivering—their sphere of soul,
And an ineffable nature-unity
They found in deepest heart of their desire
To know the Master and attain in Him.

How should He stand between them, who from vast
To vaster world of union, each with each,
Have daily, hourly travell'd? Does He come
To separate or offer surface yokes
And signs of marriage—say, in joining hands—
Like outward Masters, bound by outward ways?
Or shall He stand indeed as if without
Who dwells within? So therefore, while the rich
Experience ripen'd, magnified and grew,
They learn'd that never as that Master came
On earth would He Whom only hearts discern
Be seen by them.
                     Thus up from grade to grade
The Presence sent its splinter'd shafts above
The verge of conscious being. So it wax'd,
At first a glimmering point, a notion first,
An intuition, a new sense realized,
Then living message of unutter'd Word,
That time abiding when the twain-in-one

Should hear the Word in all its fullness spoken,
Being themselves the utterance.
       Meanwhile
Full many worshippers without the gate,
And some who went upon the quest within
Seeking a term, and some who on the call
Tarried, but ever for a Lord without
Look'd only, saw the Blessed Master stand
Between the Bearers of the Pyx and Cup,
Hailing with joyful hearts the King to be
In this most holy Church of living men.

So all about the Many-Mansion'd House
They said no longer, May Thy Kingdom come,
But bless'd the Master and the King Divine,
And all the worlds renew'd in joy with Him.

SAY: Peace be thine, when I go forth at length;
    But pray ye never for my soul's repose:
  Commend it rather to the Source of strength
 For other work, as sense of mission grows.
The ways are vast, Amen: the worlds extend
    World without end.

When after work achieved from star to star
   And all the missions in His Name fulfill'd,
God draws me where the Halls of Silence are
   And at the heart of things the soul is still'd,
Give me that active centre's rest—ah, then
    Such sleep. Amen.

XVII

Within the Veil

ON QUÆSTOR DEI and BEATA came
 So great an opening of inward ways
That when so e'er the earthly Master sat
Between them, in a silence more than words
He taught. All evil of the world within
Had pass'd from both. The very word of it
Perish'd.
 Their bodies and the needs of these
Struck in no note of discord through the pure
Tone-poem of two souls express'd henceforth
In one great organ flood of melody.
Their flesh itself, into the Law Divine
Caught up, was after its material mode
A perfect matter for the work of soul.
So clarified, so shining, so transform'd,
No outward change survened, as if a man
Should pass them and behold with normal eyes
Some sudden raying of a nimbus-light,

Or even those who shared their home and board,
Talk'd with them, took their hands or kiss'd at night
And morning. From within the change of veils
Came, and the light of it to soul alone
Was visible.
              The Master saw and knew,
Marking with joy the progress of the work,
And now upon the dual plane of life
All things grew perfect towards a perfect end.
He in rare moments, amidst the silence, seem'd
A spirit, an unembodied Word within,
Which ever on the verge of utterance
Paused, and a joy of expectation fill'd
The twain, as if he should be yet declared
In full. Moreover, if he spoke it seem'd
Ever an echo of the waited Word,
As though some virtue very far away
Its last reverberations at dim gates
Of sense expended and resounded there:
A wisdom, crown'd and clothed in regnant speech.

So were they led without in unity.
Within, without the transformation grew
And interlock'd, at once in man and maid,
All modes by which the things unseen and seen
Are realized—in flesh, in vision life
Of sleep, and in awaken'd ways of mind.

WITHIN THE VEIL

Activities of each on either side
To stillness tended, but the stillness rose
From heart and centre of activity,
An all ineffable continuance
Of vibrant being. Uplifted in the ways
Of vision through the sacred gates of sleep,
Or drawn 'twixt these again to waking life,
One life was theirs, one sense of end at hand.

But after many intervening days,
There came a Mass-Time when with Pyx and Cup
They stood before the Portal of the House,
While all the world about that sacred place,
With many known and precious from the streets
Of cities or the embosom'd country-side,
Knelt on the steps and far and far away
Stretch'd through the shining distance. Not as once
They fed them by dispensing Wine and Bread;
But Pyx and Chalice to their arms' full height
Were raised in blessing on the multitude;
And from those Sacred Vessels came a light
Which was not light but flood of life outpour'd,
Yet like a thousand suns. No word of all
The heart's high Mass-Words did the Bearers speak,
But through the still, quick air Words which were light
And Life of life spoke in the soul of each,

THE BOOK OF THE HOLY GRAAL

For Christ on that high morning was with those
Who worshipp'd. All of them received from Him
That which is He after the highest mode
Whereto the individual soul could make
An answer. So the holy work imposed
Upon the Bearers to the end thereof
Was brought. The Word received into the heart
Abode therein. The people from their knees
Rose up in silence: then a great hush'd cry
Roll'd over, echoing from end to end
And lifted quickly to a pæan's point,
An acclamation, a triumphal song,
While in the sight of that vibrating crowd
The Pyx and Chalice in a blaze of light
Were caught into the violet vault of heaven.
Together growing in the altitude
They seem'd one Cup, shone over by a Host's
White disk, which slowly—so a star might set—
Sank in the Chalice. In the rays thereof
This melted, and a Spiritual Sun
Over the Sacred Spiritual House
Ray'd, emblematic of the Sun of Christ,
And all the world beneath it burst in buds
And blossoms; all the sparkling water-ways
Scream'd music, singing of the River of Life;

And all the orchard closes glow'd and groan'd
In gladness, heavy laden with rich fruit,
Like to the Tree of Life.
                    Divested thus
The Bearers stood, with arms upon their breasts
Cross'd and heads bow'd, while on them fell the rays
Of that most glorious Sun, till every hair
Which crown'd them and their garments' every thread
Were interwoven with its aureate light.
So stood the twain transfigured, and midwise
In the first line of worshippers they saw
Their leading Master of the outward ways
Clothed in the simple habit of a monk,
Nor otherwise distinguish'd from the crowd.
But when their eyes met, then he raised his hands
In benediction, and they saw thereon
The marks stigmatic of the mastership
Shine faintly and a pallid nimbus round
His brows, but looking like a crown of thorns.
So he fell back among the crowd, which closed
About him unawares, and so they knew
Their Master's work upon the life of them
Was finish'd. Therefore in a hush of hearts
Thankful and gladden'd, conscious that they too
Relinquish'd office in that hour and place,
The twain turn'd inward and with reverent steps

Went back into the Many-Mansion'd House:
The portals closed upon them silently.

Wrapp'd in a purely spiritual state,
The House gave back to them no sense of quest,
And—they so close upon attainment's verge—
No human presence. Even theirs dissolved
Into that single mode of being-life
Which ever and again their souls had touch'd
In most deep moments. They beheld alone
The golden veil, the glory passing through
And them possessing ever more and more.
They did not seem to traverse aisle or nave;
These also had dissolved—at least for them:
Only the veil remain'd and they thereby,
As heart to heart is close—two flames of love
And white desire in utter whitest heat
Rarefied: two as one, one flame, one love
Drawn inward. Whether in or out of time
I know not, but in state which lies beyond
Duration's sense, upfolded, still'd in love,
They knew the Master and the Word Divine
With and within them.
                      Then the Golden Veil
Was parted, as another bar dissolved.
O golden light, far shining, all within:
O light beyond all light: O Life of life

And Life exceeding life: O very God
Of very God: a moment, and with eyes
Of soul, upon the object and the end
Of all soul's love they look'd. The Word made flesh
In Palestine, as prototype of all
Union between the Immanence within
The cosmos and the souls abiding there,
Shone glorious in the high heart of the light—
Spirit and soul inwoven. A time-flash,
And this had pass'd; but now—apart from form
Or aught distinguish'd as the sight of mind—
All in a keen awareness, they discern'd
The omnipresent universal soul
Of all humanity made one in Christ,
The spirit of the cosmos. This in turn
Gave way; even the universal soul
Dissolved in union with the cosmic Christ
And conscious realization therewithin.
One moment; then the Immanence Divine
Dissolved in the Divine Transcendence. Then
It was as if a Voice—which was no voice
Of earth but like the heavens together run
And flowing into utter'd harmony—
Cried All in All. And the Great Mystery
For QUÆSTOR DEI and BEATA reach'd
Its consummation. The love-object drawn
Within, to their own selves they died in love.

Their separation pass'd in mystic death,
And Godly-conscious in the Source and End,
They knew as they were known henceforth in God.

The Sacred Bread of manifested forms
And things fell, sweetly broken and dissolved,
Into the Wine-Cup of Eternal Life.

Now I, who witness in humility
Of these high things in nuptials of the soul,
Thereafter left the Holy House and came
To my own dwelling, looking to return
To-morrow as the Keeper of the Gate.

Give me that gracious morrow, Lord of All,
Or the Eternal Now attain'd in Thee.

A THOUSAND thresholds of the Church of God
    In chapels and hermit-houses by the way:
  In these as substitutes our feet have trod,
  Poor pilgrims, fain to worship, waiting day.
And the great minsters rise into the blue
    Of holy heaven, as our own hearts aspire;
The solemn Rites perform their service due,
    Recording varied notes of our desire.
O music, majesty, resounding prayer,
    Beyond the Churches that we build and see,
Beyond those forms which we have made so fair,
On some Lord's day, in spirit, transplant us where
    The Priest and Master of the Rite is He.
Lord Christ, high term of every sacred vow,
The Church within the Church—that Church is Thou.

XVII
Valete

L AST symbol, very sacrament, last type
  Before all types dissolve upon the verge
Of one unveiled reality, I bring
The speaking witness of the inward eyes
That, once encompass'd by your Godward orm,
Beheld its meanings and—from eyes to heart
More deeply held within—have known its life,
Which compasses and penetrates and fills.
A House of Many Mansions, built of God,
Wherefrom the protoplasts and types go forth;
High Palace of the Presence; fountain-point
Which sanctions delegates and calls them back,
Commissions priests and yet again withdraws
Beyond all Rites; foundation-seat of grace
Outflowing, salving the elect; and souls,
Transmuted by that grace, in fine return
Where the hush'd stillness keeps them: I, who stand
And watch and pray within the Holy Place,

Have caught beyond all voices and beyond
All image-making of your sanctuary
A wordless call to follow where it leads—
Thither whence none return. On that dread brink
I look to lay my human nature down,
Bear all I am into the All of All,
And in a last attainment of the self
Set self aside for ever. Having learn'd
The grievous lessons of the Thou and I,
Take me within, that I may know in Thee,
Lord, but in Me no more. So, standing thus
On Thine unimaged threshold—while the bonds
Begin to slip, the longing to be done
Quivers within, the deep of Thine abyss
Draws—I turn once to witness of Thy House,
For others call'd thereto. Hear in the heart,
Ye who have ears within. May open doors
Receive you, may the Temple of the Light
Lift broider'd veils and let the secret place—
Wherein the Master of the House abides—
Give up the Presence and the Mystery
Of Thee and Him, face unto face and eye
To eye. So only, never else, unfolds
The undeclared, the infinite state beyond
Both Him and Thee, God and man's end therein.

Stone Guild Publishing

Look for these and other great titles at:
http://www.stoneguildpublishing.com

Book of Ancient and Accepted Scottish Rite by Charles T. McClenachan
The Book of the Holy Graal by A. E. Waite
The Book of the Lodge by George Oliver
The Builders by Joseph Fort Newton
Chymical Marriage of Christian Rosencreutz translated by A. E. Waite
The Doctrine and Literature of the Kabalah by A. E. Waite
Fama Fraternitatis and Confession of the Rosicrucians by A. E. Waite
Freemasonry in the Holy Land by Robert Morris
The Freemason's Manual by Jeremiah How
The Freemason's Monitor by Daniel Sickels
The History of Freemasonry and Concordant Orders
The History of Initiation by George Oliver
Illustrations of the Symbols of Freemasonry by Jacob Ernst
The Kybalion by The Three Initiates
Low Twelve by Edward S. Ellis
Morals and Dogma for the 21st Century
   by Brian Chaput, William Goodell, Kevin Main, and JJ Miller
The New Masonic Trestleboard by Charles W. Moore
The Perfect Ceremonies of Craft Masonry
The Poetry of Freemasonry by Rob Morris
Real History of the Rosicrucians by A. E. Waite
The Symbolism of Freemasonry by Albert G. Mackey
Symbolism of the Three Degrees by Oliver Day Street
Taylor's Monitor by William M. Taylor
Taylor-Hamilton Monitor of Symbolic Masonry by Sam R. Hamilton
Three Hundred Masonic Odes and Poems by Rob Morris
True Masonic Chart or Hieroglyphic Monitor by Jeremy Cross

www.ingramcontent.com/pod-product-compliance
Lightning Source LLC
Chambersburg PA
CBHW060532100426
42743CB00009B/1498